PSYCHED TO WIN

Robert M. Nideffer, PhD
Professor, San Diego State University
President, Enhanced Performance Systems

Leisure Press
Champaign, Illinois

Library of Congress Cataloging-in-Publication Data

Nideffer, Robert M.
    Psyched to win / Robert M. Nideffer.
        p.   cm.
    Includes index.
    ISBN 0-88011-463-0
    1. Sports--Psychological aspects.   I. Title.
    GV706.4.N53   1992
    796'.01--dc20   91-38529
                                                              CIP

ISBN: 0-88011-463-0

Copyright © 1992 by Robert M. Nideffer

Interior photo credits: Page 1: photo of Ros Fairbank by Carol L. Newsom. Page 11: photo of Kent Ferguson courtesy of the International Swimming Hall of Fame. Page 19: photo of Joe Montana by Michael Zagarias. Page 41 by Phil Messersmit, 61 by Gary Eifert, and 69 by Lisa Davis; courtesy of *The Daily Illini*, Champaign, IL. Page 51: courtesy of Western New Mexico University. Page 77: courtesy of the Pocono Mountains Vacation Bureau. Page 85: photo of Bip Roberts courtesy of the San Diego Padres Baseball Club. Page 101: courtesy of the American Bowling Congress. Page 117: The New York Yankees' photograph of Reggie Jackson was reproduced with the permission of the New York Yankees.

Acquisitions Editor: Brian Holding
Developmental Editor: Peggy Rupert
Managing Editor: Julia Anderson
Assistant Editors: Elizabeth Bridgett, Moyra Knight, Laura Bofinger
Copyeditor: Claire Mount
Proofreader: Kari Nelson
Indexer: Sheila Ary
Production Director: Ernie Noa
Typesetting and Text Layout: Angela K. Snyder
Text Design: Keith Blomberg
Cover Design: Jack Davis
Cover Photo: Dave Black
Illustrations: Tim Offenstein
Printer: United Graphics
Printed in the United States of America
10 9 8 7 6 5 4 3 2 1

Leisure Press
A Division of Human Kinetics Publishers, Inc.
Box 5076, Champaign, IL 61825-5076
1-800-747-4457

Canada Office:
Human Kinetics Publishers, Inc.
P.O. Box 2503, Windsor, ON N8Y 4S2
1-800-465-7301 (in Canada only)

Europe Office:
Human Kinetics Publishers (Europe) Ltd.
P.O. Box IW14
Leeds LS16 6TR
England
0532-781708

CONTENTS

PREFACE

Competitive athletics has changed dramatically in the past 15 years. In the United States alone, sport is a $50-billion-a-year industry. Many professional baseball and basketball players draw salaries of $1 million to $4 million a year! At the age of 13, Jennifer Capriati signed a $3-million contract with a clothing company—before she had played her first tennis tournament as a professional.

Geographical limitations have been shattered. Even in youth sport, we see teams traveling thousands of miles to compete. Accompanying this explosion of money and the dissolving of geographical boundaries in sport has been an improved level of performance.

Motivated in the 1970s by the Olympic successes of countries like the Soviet Union and East Germany, the United States funded an Elite Athlete Development Project to provide Olympic-level competitors with the latest in sport science information, a critical step if U.S. athletes were to remain competitive. A major component of this project involved the development of athletes' psychological skills.

In the 1988 Olympic trials for the men's 100 meters, seven of the eight finalists clocked in under 10 seconds. Seven of the female finalists ran in less than 11 seconds. In sports like diving, gymnastics, and skating, we see athletes attempting moves we wouldn't have dreamed of 10 years ago. And, with the reunification of Germany, the pressure in international competition will become even more intense.

Competitors are getting bigger, stronger, faster, and quicker. It is not uncommon to see high school football lines that average 230 pounds from tackle to tackle. Fifteen years ago a center in high school basketball might be 6'4". Today, many high school guards are that tall.

Improvement in performance is not limited by age or sex. Masters level swimmers are bettering their times from high school, college, and even the Olympics. We are seeing similar phenomena in distance running. And women today are completing triathlons with times better than those of the winning men 5 years ago.

Given such statistics, we might expect to find fewer people willing to compete. But just the opposite seems to be happening. The money, travel, recognition, improved physical and emotional health, and, per-haps most importantly, self-satisfaction that come with success have turned millions of Americans into competitive athletes. We begin exercising for health or for social reasons and get caught up in the challenges, excitement, and rewards of competition.

In today's world it doesn't matter what your competitive arena—the level of performance is increasing. A few years ago you could be competitive on the basis of talent or training or coaching or mental toughness alone. You could make up for a deficit in talent by being a little tougher than the opposition. Today, everyone seems to have talent, as well as good coaching and training. More and more, the difference between winning and losing rests with psychological factors, and dozens of books have appeared on the psychology of sport in recent years.

Any mental skills training program that promises to improve performance must affect performance-relevant physiological variables. Consider a relatively simple performance situation. The speed with which an athlete can run 100 meters is determined by two physical parameters, stride length and speed of turnover. So a psychological training program designed to enhance a sprinter's performance has to affect one of these variables.

Most of the books on sport psychology promise to improve your performance, but they don't show you how to do it. They don't provide the logical link between thought processes and motor performance that makes the programs believable, and elicits from you the kind of commitment required to effect change. Meditate, learn to relax, think positive, they say, and somehow you will perform better. The implication is that the mind somehow magically controls the body, that making a mental change will automatically increase a sprinter's time.

But a performance-relevant variable is not likely to improve unless the athlete's mental skills training program focuses on that variable. This book will help you do just that, showing you how your thoughts and feelings directly affect your physiological performance in specific situations.

Most sport psych books create more problems than they solve by generating unreasonable expectations. How many of the books that you have picked up promise you a miracle? "Follow these procedures and within a day [a week, six weeks], you'll be performing 'in the zone' every time." "Kiss your distractions [frustrations, fears, tension, choking] goodbye."

You read such false promises and get the idea that confidence and performing under pressure are all-or-nothing processes. You start to believe that if you don't have faith in your abilities 100% of the time, something must be wrong with you. Books like these erode your ability to make the type of training commitment required to develop the mental skills and strength you need to be a consistent winner in today's competitive world.

This book doesn't promise you any miracles. It does show you how you can systematically develop confidence and faith in your abilities—confidence and faith that are based on results. The self-hypnosis scripts provided in this book will help you stay centered and in control in a competitive environment. I also explain how to use key or "trigger" words to help you remain focused. The final chapter is a troubleshooter's guide to overcoming problems you may encounter while developing your training program.

Focusing concentration, controlling levels of muscle tension, thinking positively under stressful competitive conditions—these are skills that can be developed. You don't just wake up with them one morning—they are skills you work to attain and that you continue to develop all of your life.

Many books treat mental skills as something to be developed apart from the actual competitive situation, perpetuating the myth that mind and body are separate. Many coaches are reluctant to introduce psychological skills training to athletes, for they have the mistaken impression that training will either take away from practice time or add to an already overcrowded schedule.

A good mental skills training program doesn't take away from practice—it improves practice quality. I show you how to apply the techniques and skills you will be learning to actual practice and competitive situations. I encourage you to bring both your mind and your body to competition! I also teach you how to use time away from the competitive environment to sharpen both your mental and your physical skills. The psychological skills training program presented in this book will teach you how to master the mental skills necessary to improve your physical performance.

CHAPTER 1

ARE YOUR PROBLEMS TECHNICAL OR PSYCHOLOGICAL?

When feelings of doubt, anxiety, tension, or frustration distract you, it's easy to lose sight of the court.

When an athlete wants to correct or improve his or her performance, he or she must first identify the source of the problem. Choosing which course of action to take is a major source of anxiety for some athletes. They must contend with conflicting ideas about what their problems are and how to solve them.

Choosing a Course of Action

Let's take the example of what appears to be a simple technical problem in tennis. John isn't happy with his serve. It doesn't have the depth and pace he would like. His coach tells him to alter his ball toss and "break his wrist more." In attempting to make these changes, John struggles and feels awkward, which leads him to doubt his coach's instructions. While John is still struggling with his serve, another coach walks by and offers him some free advice. She tells him that his hips aren't coming through and that he needs more shoulder rotation.

In addition to the advice he's received from the coaches, John might also consult a sport psychologist, who tells him that his problem is excess anxiety.

So, in attempting to improve his serve, John now must decide which, if any, of the pieces of advice he should follow. His serve is bound to improve if he follows through with any one of them, but under present conditions, he is more likely to doubt all three sets of instructions and to revert to old habits. This will become painfully clear during a match when he isn't serving well, especially if the two coaches are observing. Instead of concentrating on the game, John will be debating what to do—follow the first coach's advice, follow the second coach's advice, or try to relax. If he is like most athletes with this type of conflict, he will jump from one solution to another. Whichever way he chooses, John's game will fall apart, because none of the changes will have been practiced enough to be consistent.

In this situation, John can't help but be overloaded by the conflicting advice he's been given, as well as his own opinions. That's because he refused to fully accept any one of them and work on it. Now he doesn't know whom to place his confidence in. To make matters worse, he feels trapped—if he goes with any one person's advice, the other two people are likely to resent it.

You must take responsibility for choosing and following through on a course of action.

John wants to improve his serve, but he can't do this unless he makes a commitment to a specific course of action. Jumping from one solution to another is just looking for miracles and will never lead to consistent and improved performance.

As an athlete, it is your responsibility to either decide what your problem is and how you're going to solve it, or put your faith in someone else to do this for you. In either case, you have to believe in and follow through with your course of action.

Making a choice and having faith in that choice helps you quiet the voice of doubt and conflict in your mind.

Once you make a choice that you really believe in, the doubts you have about whose advice to follow disappear. Once you commit to a course of action, you have already made tremendous progress even though you haven't yet changed anything physical about your game. You have already improved your ability to concentrate by removing some of the internal distractions that kept you from concentrating on the things you should focus on (e.g., the ball).

Now, what can you do to develop faith in your choice? The first task is to be sure that you have accurately identified your problem. You must decide whether the problem is one of concentration and arousal control (psychological) or one requiring technical and/or tactical changes.

How Do You Know When the Problem Is Psychological?

The techniques and procedures in this book have been designed to help you control concentration and physiological arousal, because that is the psychological key to reaching your peak performance state, or playing "in the zone." These techniques assume that you are not playing up to your potential.

How do you know that your problem stems from a loss of control over your physiological arousal or ability to concentrate, and isn't simply a technical or tactical mistake? It isn't always easy to separate these factors. For example, loss of control over physiological arousal results in changes in muscle tension that can dramatically affect your coordination and timing. However, many observers would identify the problem as technical (especially coaches, who have been trained to look for technical problems.)

When muscles are tight in tennis, for example, you can't move quickly enough, get low enough for shots, "crack your wrist on serve," and get your weight going through the ball. When feelings of doubt, anxiety, tension, or frustration distract you, it's easy to lose sight of the court. If you can't see what is going on, you can't play smart (tactical) tennis. If you can't see the ball, your preparation is going to be late. Technical problems occur because you aren't reacting quickly enough. You find yourself falling backwards, hitting the ball off your back foot, and not taking the volleys "out in front."

Under the conditions just described, you would probably get a lot of technical instructions from your coach to improve your game. Will those technical instructions make a difference? Are technical problems the real issue? The following questions should help you distinguish between the technical and the psychological aspects of your performance.

1. Are you satisfied with your skill level when you are playing well? If not, then you probably don't have the skill level necessary to play up to your potential. You need to develop greater strength, speed, and coordination and maybe alter your technique. The best way to do this is through physical practice. No amount of mental rehearsal will help you perform well if you lack technical skill. There is no substitute for actual practice.

2. Do mistakes occur randomly, or do they increase in pressure situations? A purely technical problem will occur in a wide variety of situations. In golf, for example, you may have a technical problem that leads to slicing the ball. This will occur fairly constantly, or on a random basis. You will not be able to see a pattern to the problem (e.g., slicing only in pressure situations). When the problem is psychological, the mistakes will tend to occur more frequently under pressure, and they will have a predictable pattern. In the golf example, some golfers might tend to leave putts short or string together two or more bad shots (allowing the first error to affect concentration on the second shot) when money is riding on the outcome.

3. When you are having a problem, how do you feel? If you feel confident and in control of your thoughts and feelings, then the problem may involve nothing more than a simple technical issue. If you feel a sense of panic, if you feel pressured and rushed, as if you weren't being given enough time to get ready, or if you feel confused and overloaded, not sure what to do, chances are the problem is primarily psychological.

4. Is the problem affecting only one aspect of your performance, or are several things going wrong at the same time? When stress is a factor, the increase in muscle tension interferes with your vision and concentration. Under stressful conditions, you are not likely to be dealing with a single problem (e.g., low ball toss on a serve in tennis). Instead, you will find that everything is going wrong. The tennis player's double faults increase the pressure and affect other aspects of his or her game (e.g., tightening up on ground strokes and volleys). The golfer's poor putts lead to increased tension on subsequent shots as he or she tries to make up for each mistake.

These four questions are important, and we will return to them on the following pages. Your answers will help you develop faith in the particular approach that you take to solving your performance problems.

Distinguishing Between Technical and Psychological Problems: Two Examples

Let's say that you are a hitter in baseball. You've been up to bat twice and struck out both times, swinging late at the ball and not adjusting to the speed of the pitch. After the second strikeout the hitting coach says that you were "wrapping your bat" too far behind your head. All you have to do is correct that technical error, and you won't be late on the swing.

You listen to the advice and then ask yourself each of the four questions listed previously. In response to Question 1, you remind yourself that you have been hitting the ball well and are satisfied with your skill level (i.e., you know you can hit against this pitcher).

In answer to Question 2, you decide that the situations during which the two strikeouts occurred weren't particularly stressful. The first strikeout occurred in the first inning: The score was still 0-0, and there wasn't anyone on base. The second strikeout occurred in the third inning: Your team was ahead 3-0, there were two outs, and no one was on base. It seems clear that the mistakes were more likely random occurrences.

You remember that you felt comfortable and confident in the batter's box (Question 3). You had no trouble seeing the ball and watching it leave the pitcher's hand. You didn't feel pressured or rushed; instead, you just weren't "getting around on the pitch."

Finally, when you consider Question 4, you decide that the rest of your game was going well. You hadn't made any fielding errors, missed any signs, or lost control of your emotions. So the answers to all four questions suggest that you may very well be dealing with a technical problem, as your coach had said.

In this situation the obvious solution is to make the technical correction that seems to be indicated. Fortunately, in baseball you can get away with focusing on making a technical correction during a game because you have time to think and make adjustments after each swing. The same isn't true in sports where you have an opponent who keeps making you react. A tennis player, for example, often has to hit a ball several times in a rally. A boxer can't take one swing and then call time out. If your technical correction keeps you from concentrating on other aspects of the sport, then you will have to wait and make the correction in practice instead of during a game.

Let's look at an example from tennis that is more complicated than the baseball problem described previously. Assume that you have started to double-fault on your serve. You examine the problem by asking yourself the four questions, but none of your answers is clear-cut. You think you have a good, but inconsistent, serve and aren't satisfied with your ball toss (Question 1). You admit that you double-faulted twice, perhaps because you were under pressure, but point out that it's still early in the match and things could change (Question 2). You admit that you really don't know how you feel (Question 3). (It's at least clear that you're not feeling confident, or you would say so.) Finally, you indicate that you haven't noticed any other problems during the match (Question 4). If you can get your serve straightened out, then everything else will fall into place.

In all of these responses, you have avoided making a decision. You hedge your bets by responding that your problem might be psychological, but it might also be technical. This enables you to believe that you might be able to correct your mistakes by making a technical change—something many athletes view as easier than dealing with a psychological problem. If the mistake is technical, then all the athlete need do is learn the proper technique and make the adjustment, and, like magic, everything will work out.

Reluctance to Admit a Psychological Problem Exists

For many coaches and athletes, technical problems are easier to accept than psychological ones. Problems associated with control of concentration and arousal are seen by some as evidence of a lack of motivation, laziness, vulnerability, a bad attitude, and the like. In reality, psychological problems occur because a person hasn't developed psychological skills, just as technical problems occur when he or she lacks technical skills. People have attitude and/or motivational problems when they have the physical and psychological skills necessary to control their behaviors, but consciously refuse to do so. They are lazy when they know what they need to work on, but refuse to do it.

Most of the concentration and arousal problems that I see occur because athletes haven't learned the proper skills, not because they lack motivation, are lazy, or have attitude problems. As you will see in subsequent chapters, once you discipline yourself to learn proper psychological techniques, problems with concentration and arousal can be remedied as easily as the technical problems that creep into your performance routine can be changed. Once you accept the fact that control over concentration and arousal is a skill, just like control over motor responses, you can overcome your reluctance to recognize and accept psychological problems.

When in doubt, try making a technical adjustment.

Let's return to our last example in which you have double-faulted during a match. If you come to me for help, I would consider your answers and conclude that your problem was not technical, but psychological. That conclusion would be based on the fact that you lacked confidence leading to a loss of concentration and control over arousal, which ultimately interfered with your service motion.

However, this analysis is inconclusive for me as well as for you. I don't see a clear pattern, and the rest of your game is not affected.

Without being positive, and without being able to convince you the problem was a psychological one, I would tell you that it might be psychological but would encourage you to go ahead and try to solve the problem technically. Then, if a simple technical solution didn't work, that fact would provide both of us with convincing evidence that the problem is indeed psychological. Thus, the failure to make a technical correction would lead to increased confidence in the necessity of developing your psychological skills.

When the problem is psychological, but a technical solution is attempted in practice, there is usually an immediate improvement. This is because the stress that has been interfering with concentration and technique has been removed. Unfortunately, the improvement disappears as soon as the pressure of competition is reapplied.

When the problem is psychological, but a technical solution is attempted during competition, performance often gets worse. The reason for this can be seen in the tennis example. Say you decide that you can correct your double faults by controlling your toss and that if you concentrate on achieving a certain toss motion, the ball will always land where you want it to. What you will discover, however, is that tennis requires rapid shifts in attention. If you focus your concentration on one aspect of your game (e.g., your ball toss), you won't be able to shift your focus and prepare quickly enough for your next shot. Serve and volley players who are struggling with their serves often find themselves not getting to the net quickly enough, not taking the volleys out in front, and not anticipating where their opponents' returns will be.

Playing in the zone in tennis means rapidly shifting from a broad-external focus of concentration (i.e., the whole court) when the ball is on the other side of the net, to a narrow focus (i.e., the ball) as the ball crosses to your side.

If you can confine the technical correction on the toss to a simple reminder (e.g., toss the ball to a certain spot), and you have practiced the proper move over and over, you can probably make the correction without major difficulties and get into the zone. Problems will arise, however, if you are trying something new or have to monitor the entire toss.

When your technical solution fails your only hope is to build faith in a psychological intervention.

Practice is the place to try new things, develop new techniques, and work on those techniques until they can be performed automatically. If you are having problems during a competition, and the obvious technical solution doesn't work, you must stop trying to make technical corrections and concentrate instead on gaining control over concentration and arousal. This is the key to improving your performance.

Summary

For any mental skills training program to be effective you must be committed and practice. It's impossible to commit to a training program, however, if you aren't sure that it's the right one. Often, athletes have difficulty deciding if their problem is psychological or technical. This doubt causes them to waver between different strategies and, as a result, they fail to make the changes needed to improve performance.

To reduce the inner voices of doubt that keep you from making the kind of commitment required to be successful, you must decide for yourself if the problem is psychological. Chances are the problem is psychological if

1. you are satisfied with your level of skill when you are playing well,
2. mistakes tend to occur more frequently under pressure,
3. you find yourself having a lot of negative thoughts or feelings during the performance, and
4. a breakdown in one area leads to other problems as well.

CHAPTER 2

ALTERED STATES
OF CONSCIOUSNESS

**There was nothing he had to consciously do to
maintain control; the dive became automatic.**

I was warming up and made a decision to perform
a reverse dive with one-half twist in a layout position. It's a very pretty dive when done well, and one
I enjoy. You begin the dive by taking a normal
approach to the end of the diving board—the same
approach that you would use for a simple front dive.
Then, as you spring up into the air, you reverse your
direction, diving backwards toward the board. At
the very top of the dive you should be in an upside-
down swan-dive position, with your head and back
over the diving board. At that point, if you were to
drop straight down, you would hit your head on the
board. From this position, your body pivots and you

drop one shoulder, twisting so that you end up just missing the board and entering the water headfirst with your back toward the diving board. It's a pretty dive all right, but it can be frightening because the first part of it is blind—that is, you can't see the board or the water.

On this particular occasion, I came up off the board in perfect position. It was as though something had clicked inside me. I knew exactly where my body was relative to the board, even though I couldn't see it. I had perfect control over my body and crystal-clear, complete awareness of what was going on. Time seemed slowed down as if everything was happening in slow motion. I floated up, up, up, and as I reached the very top of the dive, I seemed to hang in the air. I knew that a good portion of my body was over the board, and I knew that I would miss hitting the board by about 3 inches. As I began to drop a shoulder and twist, I heard the screams of the crowd (they thought I was going to hit the board). As I was twisting, my eyes went past the people and I saw very clearly the expressions on their faces and the fear in their eyes. I instinctively smiled, feeling such power and control. I exulted in knowing exactly where I was—and in thrilling the crowd. I turned my body and dropped 3 inches from the board to complete what had to be one of the most perfect dives of my life.

This description illustrates a peak experience, or altered state of consciousness. The dive and the changes in perception associated with it are nearly identical to the changes that a tennis player or basketball player feels as he or she plays in the zone. Similar alterations occur in baseball, shooting, and other sports when athletes tell you that objects seemed bigger, that they knew they would get a hit, or that they couldn't possibly miss a target.

Although the experience is common to virtually every imaginable sport, it is not common to a particular athlete. Relatively few athletes can create a peak experience or get into the zone at will. For the majority, getting into the zone occurs spontaneously in response to uncontrolled environmental conditions rather than factors that each athlete consciously controls!

Taking Advantage of Your Psychological Strengths

Has anyone ever told you that *you are playing at 10 percent of your ability*? You might even have said this to others. We make this statement because every once in a while we play in the zone. Such performances give us a glimpse of our potential and allow us to dream about what it would be like to play that way all the time.

Now, no scientific study exists that proves how much of our abilities we are using. Such a study would have to account for the tremendous differences that exist across individuals. But the issue isn't whether you are playing at 10 percent or 95 percent of your ability. Neither does it concern whether psychological factors account for 5 percent or 95 percent of winning and losing. The real issue is learning to take full advantage of your psychological strengths to perform at a higher, more consistent level.

One of the reasons coaches and athletes are less developed in their psychological skills than in their physical, technical, and tactical skills is that they haven't been given the necessary information to develop them. When an athlete wants to improve physical strength in a particular muscle group, he or she knows the amount of weight to lift, the muscle group to use, and the number of repetitions required. In addition, all athletes have obvious ways of measuring success in acquiring physical or technical skills. In the weight-lifting example, they see some fairly immediate changes in strength. And because the information they have been provided with makes sense, they can understand the relationship between work and muscle strength and between strength and improved performance.

Sport psychology has yet to provide coaches and athletes with the operational definitions they need to build faith in various psychological interventions. We tell people to concentrate, to believe, to be confident, to be mentally tough, but most of the time we don't tell them how, and we don't show the link between their thoughts and their performance.

More and more athletes are turning to mental rehearsal to improve performance, but few can tell you why the procedures they are using are supposed to help. Under these circumstances, it is not surprising that few athletes adhere to any particular mental training program for very long.

Psychology has advanced to such a point that we can begin to define what we mean by *concentration*. We now understand enough about human consciousness and altered states of consciousness to explain how changes in perception affect human performance. We can tell you what is happening both when you have a peak experience and when you "choke." In addition, we can identify the particular attentional processes involved. Finally, we can give you specific exercises to gain greater control over these processes. To make use of this knowledge, you must first understand what an altered state of consciousness (ASC) is.

Altered States of Consciousness in Sport

During the 1960s the increased use of mind-altering drugs like marijuana and lysergic acid (LSD) generated a great deal of interest in the study of human consciousness. In particular, investigators became interested in operationally defining alterations in normal awareness. For example, how does a person receive and process information when asleep as opposed to when awake? How about when under the influence of a drug like LSD? Are there similarities between peak experiences in sport and LSD-induced alterations?

Ludwig (1969) examined a wide variety of ASC experiences including dreams, drug experiences, meditation, spontaneous peak experiences, and mental disturbances. By carefully analyzing the subjective descriptions of these different states, he identified specific perceptual and information processing skills that seemed to be critical determinants of these experiences. A list of the characteristics of an ASC is found in Table 2.1. Though ASC experiences will differ depending on the context and the individual, Table 2.1 provides a general idea of the characteristics that are found across a variety of experiences. Not every characteristic will be associated with every ASC, but a great deal of overlap exists. For example, almost every ASC experience involves a time distortion and a perceptual distortion.

The diving example from the beginning of this chapter fits the general pattern listed in Table 2.1. In a normal state of consciousness a diver is aware of the board, the dive, and the water. In the dive described, the diver was aware of everything in the pool area. Time was distorted as he "floated up, up, up, ... and seemed to hang in the air."

Unlike the ASC described in Table 2.1, the diver did not sense a loss of control—rather, he felt as if he had total control. Emotionally, he "exulted," feeling a sense of power and joy. However, there was nothing he had to consciously do to maintain this control. Once something clicked inside him, he knew he was in perfect position. The dive became automatic, not requiring any adjustments or corrections. He was free to observe not only

Table 2.1   Characteristics of an Altered State of Consciousness

1. *Alterations in thinking*: Subjective disturbances in attention, memory, and judgment.
2. *Disturbed time sense*: Feelings of timelessness or of the rapid acceleration of time.
3. *Loss of control*: A sense of loosing grip on reality. Shift from internal to external locus of control.
4. *Change in emotional expression:* Emotions become more or less intense than normal.
5. *Body image change*: May be a feeling of separation of mind and body (out-of-body experience). The person may become a passive observer of his or her own performance.
6. *Perceptual distortions*: Hypersensitivity to visual and kinesthetic cues; hallucinations.
7. *Changes in meaning and/or significance:* Events, experiences, ideas, and perceptions may become intense revelations.
8. *Sense of the ineffable*: An inability to adequately express what has happened.
9. *Feelings of rejuvenation*: A new sense of hope. A rebirth is often felt to have occurred.
10. *Hypersuggestibility*: Increased responsivity to suggestions, whether given implicitly or explicitly.

the dive, but everything else around the pool, including the faces in the crowd. This is likened to the body image change listed in Table 2.1

The diver's perceptions were enhanced: He saw things more clearly and was extremely sensitive to sounds and facial expressions, but not in a way that negatively affected his performance. Finally, after the dive, he experienced a sense of rejuvenation, and his motivation was extremely high.

Choking Is an Altered State of Consciousness

Many experiences lead to alterations in your normal state of consciousness. A peak experience in sport is one example of a spontaneous ASC experience. Many others, however, are more systematically induced. You experience an ASC when you dream or take drugs such as LSD, marijuana, mescaline, amphetamines, cocaine, and barbiturates. In addition, meditation, hypnosis, self-hypnosis, sensory deprivation (e.g., flotation tanks), and prayer can all be used to generate ASC experiences.

Before you get too enthusiastic about ASC experiences, however, you should know that they aren't all like playing in the zone. Experiments with hallucinogenic chemicals like LSD, DMT, and mescaline have led to some pretty frightening and destructive experiences for some individuals. In the 1960s some people claimed LSD led to oneness with God. Still others claimed that it led to a mental institution. Controlled ASC experiences are usually quite positive, but if you lose control, they can be very upsetting. Let me give you another sports example.

> I was a little anxious before the match, but I didn't feel all that bad. I kept telling myself that Tracy was the Number 1 ranked tennis player in the world, and that I didn't have anything to lose. It was a huge opportunity for me. My family and friends were there, and I was really looking forward to it. I wouldn't have minded the loss if I had played well, but this was awful. I remember feeling so upset and embarrassed midway through the second set that I was just praying that the ground would open up and

swallow me. I didn't think I could ever look anyone in the face again.

It started in the second game of the first set. I had served first and held. I had played solidly, nothing brilliant. Tracy had missed a couple of returns and it was 1-love to me. Then, in the second game I tried to come in on a second serve. I knew that to stay in the match I had to get to net, and I had to pressure her. I had hit a great return, forcing her to reach for a forehand. I had an easy "high sitter" that I should have put away. I rushed it badly, hitting it into the bottom of the net. It was all downhill from there.

I tried to come in one more time in that game and was passed easily. That was the last time I tried to get to net. In the third game, I started double-faulting. I was so worried about her returns that I couldn't think. I wasn't seeing the court; I was feeling rushed and I panicked.

I couldn't concentrate—my mind kept jumping from one thought to another. I felt confused and overloaded; I kept trying to figure things out and just couldn't. She never gave me enough time. I would get back to return serve and the ball would be there before I was ready. I was late on everything, spraying balls all over the place.

At one point I was feeling so much tension in my body that I was afraid I wouldn't even be able to swing my racquet on serve. I didn't know if I would get the ball in play. In fact, there was one point where I double-faulted and the ball didn't even get to the net. You can ask me what happened, but I can't really remember too much. I don't have a clue as to what she was doing. I don't think I even saw her side of the court. I hope I never have another day like that!

The experience just described is a classic example of what happens when an athlete chokes. Fortunately, those experiences don't occur every day—if they did, athletic careers would be much shorter. Choking is the athlete's equivalent to a bad trip on LSD, and it, too, can be considered an ASC.

Comparing the athlete's description with the characteristics presented in Table 2.1, you can see how her normal state of consciousness was altered. She couldn't concentrate and was unable to engage in normal problem solving. Time sped up instead of slowing down. She felt rushed, as if there weren't enough time to prepare. She had lost control of her thoughts, her behavior, and the entire situation.

Emotionally, she was panicked and all her feelings were intensified ("I wanted the ground to swallow me up"). She was out of touch with her own body. Timing and coordination were off, and she couldn't feel the ball against the racquet. She was insensitive to many of the visual cues that she needed to be aware of, including her opponent, the ball, and the court. This wasn't just a loss, it was a disaster. The athlete was extremely responsive to any negative cue. The slightest hint that she might not be playing well (i.e., the first missed volley) resulted in an emotional overreaction.

Summary

Both playing in the zone and choking are examples of phenomena that psychologists refer to as *altered states of consciousness* (ASC). Any time you experience an extraordinary change in perception of time, ability to remember and think, feelings, and/ or responsivity to suggestions, you experience an altered state of consciousness.

If you have had the experience of playing in the zone or of choking, then you have already seen that you are capable of developing an altered state of consciousness. If you have had either of these experiences you are capable of learning to use self-hypnosis to gain greater control over your concentration and performance.

CHAPTER 3

UNDERSTANDING THE NATURE OF HUMAN CONSCIOUSNESS

The defensive line begins to move around, forcing Montana to broaden his attention, reassess the situation, momentarily analyze it, and decide whether to alter the play he has called.

It should now be obvious that you have the potential for altering your normal state of consciousness. You can speed up and slow down your perception of the passage of time. You can alter your emotions and remain calm in the face of incredible pressure or stress. And finally, you can push yourself to emotional highs and drop yourself into extreme lows.

People have attempted to explain ASCs in a variety of ways. Although many of these explanations are based on religious or mystical ideas, it's clear that altered states aren't the work of spirits. We can't point to the exact spot in the brain where they occur, or identify the specific biochemical changes that account for what is going on, but we have enough "circumstantial" evidence to place a great deal of confidence in less superstitious and more scientific explanations of what is going on. Research on the effects of arousal on physiological and perceptual processes provides very strong evidence that human attentional processes play a critical role in the development of ASC experiences (see "References and Suggested Readings" at the end of this book). In sport, they play a critical role in the development of both experiencing a peak performance and choking.

The next section describes how your attentional focus affects your perception of time, emotions, and physical reactions. As your acceptance and understanding of this material grows, so will your commitment to gaining greater control over concentration and arousal. It is the commitment to change that will allow you to achieve your full potential as an athlete.

The Four Types of Attentional Focus

Sport psychologists now understand a great deal about the mental demands that sports situations place on athletes. For example, we now know that, rather than relying on one level of concentration, athletes engage in at least four different types of concentration (see Figure 3.1). They have a *broad-internal* focus when they need to think, plan, and analyze. The attentional focus is broad so that athletes can attend to a lot of things at once, and the direction of the focus is internal because that is where processing of information (analyzing) must take place. This analytical thinking is shown in the bottom left quadrant of Figure 3.1.

At other times an athlete needs to assess situations and be tuned in to the competitive environment. Because assessment involves a broad focus of attention (e.g., to see the whole court in tennis or the entire playing field in baseball), and because you cannot assess what is going on around you if you focus on what's occurring inside your head, this is called a *broad-external* focus of attention. The top left quadrant in Figure 3.1 illustrates some of the external cues that compete for our attention. Somehow, we have to be able to rapidly assess a broad range of external cues and then instinctively select those that are task relevant.

Figure 3.1
The four types of attentional focus.

The third type of concentration involves narrowing attention and directing it internally. We use *narrow-internal* focus of attention to systematically rehearse a performance before we actually engage in it (see the bottom right quadrant of Figure 3.1).

The fourth type of concentration is a *narrow-external* focus of attention. Athletes need this focus when they attempt to react or perform. It is reflected in the eyes of a good hitter in baseball when he is trying to hit the ball (see the top right quadrant of Figure 3.1), the intense concentration of a sprinter in the starting blocks, and the facial expression of a boxer as he throws a punch.

During normal state of consciousness, you are constantly moving from one type of attentional focus to another. Let's see how this works in the following example.

Joe Montana, quarterback of the San Francisco 49'ers has to prepare for next week's football game. He begins by watching game films of the opposing team. As he watches the films (broad-external focus), he notices differences in defensive alignments, as well as certain players' strengths and weaknesses. He shifts his attention to a broad-internal focus as he begins to analyze his own game and the relative strengths and weaknesses of the 49'ers in comparison to those of the opposition. Through this analysis he develops a game plan, deciding which plays are most likely to work under what conditions.

During the week he goes out and begins to practice for the game. Throughout the practice he runs the same plays over and over again, narrowing his focus of attention (i.e., not considering all possible options) to prepare for specific situations. During this practice he is shifting from a narrow-internal focus as he mentally rehearses a given play (i.e., just before executing it), to a narrow-external focus as he executes it. He practices beyond the point of simply being able to execute the play; he "over learns" all of the required performance skills. He does this because he wants to be able to respond automatically (without conscious thought) to certain defensive alignments on game day. By doing his conscious thinking and planning now (narrow-internal), he will have less of it to do during the game. It is the over learning that will allow him to maintain an external focus of concentration, reacting instinctively under pressure.

Montana experienced several attentional shifts in this example. These shifts, however, occurred over a long period of time. Because Montana could think and practice at his own speed (i.e., no one was pressing him to move on before he was ready), he could become immersed in one type of concentration. On game day, however, things change and attentional shifts must occur more quickly.

On Sunday he enters the game and quickly looks across the line to see what the defensive alignment is (broad-external). His pregame preparation has provided him with certain expectations and critical cues to look for. If he sees what he expects to see, he calls a play that he's been practicing all week (an automatic choice). If he sees something different, he must quickly shift attention and reanalyze things (broad-internal). Once his analysis is complete, he selects a play and begins to call the signals (narrow-external focus).

Suddenly the defensive line begins to move around, forcing Montana to again broaden his attention. He has to reassess the situation (broad-external), and momentarily analyze it (broad-internal) as he decides whether or not to alter the play he has called. He tries to complete the reassessment and analysis while he is calling the signals. If he has prepared for the movement of the defensive line, the analysis is almost automatic (i.e., requiring little conscious thought), and his attention narrows again to receive the snap from the center. If he hasn't prepared, he may find himself feeling confused and begin to tighten up physically as his arousal increases. He may need to call time-out to give himself time to calm down and reorganize.

Although a play in football requires a brief period of time, it is not unusual for concentration to shift several times during the play. Shifts in attentional focus occur in virtually every sport situation during an athlete's normal state of consciousness. Tennis players shift from a narrow to a broad and back to a narrow focus as they serve and then move to the net to execute a volley. Basketball players shift from a broad to a narrow focus several times as they move down the floor.

Playing in the zone occurs when you become immersed in an external or internal focus of attention.

One other idea needs to be brought up at this point. There are times when an athlete becomes immersed in one particular attentional focus (e.g., when Joe Montana reviewed game films). This happens because a breakdown occurs in the normal amount of shifting from an external to an internal focus of attention that goes on. Individuals experience alterations in normal consciousness whenever they become immersed in either an external or an internal focus of attention. When you are playing in the zone, your attentional shifts decrease and your focus of attention becomes much more (though not completely) external. You may shift attention from a broad to a narrow focus, but you spend very little time "in your head" either rehearsing or analyzing. When you choke, your focus is almost exclusively internal.

How Changes in Attention Lead to ASC Experiences

Table 2.1 presented some of the characteristics associated with alterations in your normal state of consciousness. This section draws upon that information, as well as the four types of attentional focus, to explain how changes in attention lead to ASC experiences.

Disturbed Time Sense

Perhaps the most common aspect of an ASC is a distorted sense of the passage of time. Athletes describe their peak experiences as involving a slowing down of time. This contrasts with the extremely rapid passage of time that we experience when we sleep or when we feel rushed and panicked because we are performing poorly (choking).

Athletes associate a certain amount of time with the various activities they engage in. For example, a baseball player sees a baseball approach at a certain rate of speed. He knows how long it takes for the ball to get from the pitcher's mound to home plate. That time estimate, however, is affected by the player's normal tendency to shift from an external to an internal focus of attention several times within the brief span of time it takes for the ball to get to the plate.

On an average day at the plate, even a great hitter like Tony Gwynn of the San Diego Padres will be fleetingly distracted several times during the length of time that it takes for the baseball to reach the plate. Those brief distractions can be external (e.g., seeing movement in fielders, base runners, or umpires) or internal (e.g., being aware of muscle tension in shoulders or arms). These types of distractions are task-irrelevant shifts in attention that interfere only slightly with the athlete's ability to stay focused on the ball.

The previous example involved a very brief time span, but the same thing applies over much longer periods. For example, during a 30-minute commute from home to work, you consciously shift your attention back and forth from things going on around you (external) to those happening within (internal).

Your estimate of the passage of time is based upon the frequency with which you shift from an external to an internal focus of attention. When you become immersed in the world around you, you stop focusing on internal concerns and instead react automatically. Your sustained external focus means you spend more real time attending to task-relevant cues (e.g., the ball).

Under these conditions, time appears to be slowed down, and you are no longer bothered by task-irrelevant distractions.

Athletes who have had peak experiences typically indicate that they were totally immersed in the experience. Rather than consciously controlling their performances, they simply let them happen. They've stopped shifting to the kind of focus that is associated with conscious analyzing (broad-internal) and rehearsing (narrow-internal). With fewer internal distractions, time seems to be slowed down.

In contrast, when athletes become immersed in their own thought processes, such as when they sleep, or when they become anxious about their performances, they stop attending to environmental cues and time seems to speed up. An individual wakes up after 8 hours of sleep feeling as if only minutes have passed. The tennis match is over before the player even got started.

The easiest way to understand the immersion process is to think of an athlete's eyes as a movie camera taking pictures of everything the individual consciously directs his or her attention to. Under normal conditions (a few fleeting internal distractions), Tony Gwynn's camera-like eyes take 20 pictures of the ball from the time it leaves the pitcher's hand until it crosses the plate. When Tony is in the zone there are fewer than normal internal distractions and his camera eyes are free to take more pictures of the ball (e.g., 30). When Tony is anxious and feeling pressure, there are more internal distractions, which results in fewer pictures than normal (e.g., 10) because the camera becomes focused on irrelevant distractions.

By decreasing distractions and becoming immersed in an external focus, Tony alters the passage of time. The ball seems to be coming toward him at a slower speed and he feels much more in control. In contrast, any reduction in Tony's ability to focus on the ball will cause him to feel as if things are happening more quickly than usual and he will have less control.

Positive and Negative Immersion

The preceding paragraphs emphasized that when you are actually playing in the zone, you are immersed in the performance situation, spending less and less time in your head. This doesn't mean that you aren't analyzing the situation, but you do this at a preconscious level. Imagine that your brain is functioning like a radar screen. The line on the radar screen that moves in a 360-degree arc is constantly searching for the unexpected. If nothing is encountered, the scanning continues uninterrupted. Once a blip appears on the screen, however, some conscious analysis must take place. When you are in the zone, everything is going according to plan. All of the feedback that you are getting tells you that you can continue to function automatically or unconsciously.

I have also suggested that choking results when you become internally immersed in task-irrelevant cues. Although this is true, it is important to note that internal immersion is not always negative. Neither is external immersion always positive. In either case, the value of the experience is determined by whether or not the cues you are attending to are task relevant. For example, the mental training procedures introduced later in this book require you to become internally immersed. When you are mentally rehearsing a performance or working out a game plan, it is appropriate for you to stop attending to the environment. In this case, you are focusing on task-relevant cues, and internal immersion is positive. Negative external immersion occurs when an athlete becomes overly upset by an official's call or loses his or her temper. This person would be better off shifting attention internally long enough to regain control.

The obvious implication for athletes who want to play in the zone is this: They first must develop their physical skills to the point where the need to shift attention from an external to an internal focus is reduced or eliminated. In other words, they must be capable of performing automatically.

Alterations in Memory

As with distortions in time, shifting attention from an external to an internal focus is a critical factor in either inhibiting or enhancing memory. This makes sense if you think of your memory as a combination of a short- and a long-term storage area. Placing information in a long-term memory storage area requires a conscious internal focus of attention.

As information comes into the brain, it is briefly stored in a short-term memory storage area, where it is made available for processing. If it is not processed and referred to long-term storage, the next information to come into short-term memory simply replaces it. The first set of information to be placed in the short-term memory is now lost from the system and cannot be recalled.

During peak experiences in sport, athletes often report losing their memories for much of the performance, and individuals who have made world-record efforts frequently remember little about their record-setting performance. This is particularly true in events requiring a narrow focus of attention (e.g., throwing the javelin, diving).

Under normal circumstances, an athlete tends to shift his or her attention back and forth from an internal to an external focus frequently during a performance. This is true even in events that don't last very long. Let's go back to a diving example. A diver completes a dive off a 3-meter board in about 3 seconds and typically shifts his or her attention several times during that period. When performance is less than perfect, this shifting is necessary, because the athlete must react to both internal and external cues (e.g., the speed of rotation is too slow or too fast, or there is too much lean at the start of the dive).

These normal shifts in attention, and the conscious processing of information that follows, result in the storing of performance information in long-term memory. A near-perfect performance alleviates the need to process information, and therefore the individual has no recall. It might be easier to understand this if you think of dreams and why it's hard to remember some of them. Basically, you have little recall because you don't consciously process your dreams. Rather, you are a participant. The dreams you remember have been consciously analyzed while they were in process. The moment you become an observer to, as well as a participant in, your dreams (e.g., thinking as you dream, "Am I dreaming?" or "This is terrible"), you consciously process them and store them in long-term memory.

Enhanced recall occurs when this process is reversed. When you focus attention internally to remember something, you can become immersed in that internal focus. If you don't shift attention back to the environment (or do so only infrequently), you will probably enhance the vividness of your memories. Internal immersion in images helps you gain greater control over both concentration and arousal. Self-hypnosis, most forms of meditation, and mental rehearsal procedures all rely on internal immersion.

As you become internally immersed you are more likely to discover memory cues that will help you locate things in long-term storage. Many individuals with memory problems learn strategies to help them retrieve information. When they can't remember where they've left something, they engage in a logical search, asking questions of themselves to stimulate recall. For example, you create images of the last things you remember to see if those images help you locate stored memories. As you recall a few bits and pieces of the actual memory, you create a framework that then allows you to fill in the memory gaps by recalling information from other situations or experiences. Just as a paleontologist might recreate an entire dinosaur from a few bones, you can use self-hypnosis to recreate past experiences from relatively few cues. It's important to remember, however, that recreating past experiences is not completely reliable. It's possible to make mistakes when you fill in the gaps.

Perceptual Distortions

We now know that immersion can enhance or inhibit recall, but it can also dramatically distort your perception. Let's return to the example of dreams to clarify this point. When sleeping, you don't shift your attentional focus as frequently. Although you are still aware of some environmental cues, this awareness is reduced. It is quite likely that the bizarre or nightmarish quality of some of your dreams is a direct consequence of this failure to shift attention to external cues.

Try to remember what it was like to be afraid of the dark or alone on a dark road at night. Perhaps you saw a shadow and became frightened. Your mind raced as you began to imagine what that shadow was. The more anxious you became, the more your attention focused internally, the more you became immersed in your own thoughts, and the more exaggerated your fantasies became. It wasn't until you broke out of your thoughts, directed your attention to the environment, and discovered what the cause of the shadow was, that reality returned. Without shifting to an external focus, normal controls over perception are interfered with and fantasy takes over. Your mind becomes self-stimulating and you start recalling images, feelings, and ideas, treating them as if they were real. Your inner world becomes your reality, and, in this anxious state, you lose control.

This same process seems to be operating when athletes choke under pressure. Recall the example of the tennis player who described choking in a match earlier in this chapter. Her growing anxiety caused her to become internally immersed in negative thoughts. Those thoughts became her reality, a self-fulfilling prophecy. When she stopped attending to the environment, she couldn't possibly perform well.

Hallucinations, Flashbacks, and Physiological Alterations

I am undoubtedly stretching things to try to use the concept of immersion to explain hallucinations, flashbacks, and some of the physiological changes that are often associated with an ASC experience. Still, I believe this idea deserves some attention. Immersion provides a more rational explanation for some of the startling phenomena that are associated with ASCs than many of the other hypotheses that have been offered.

Pavlov, in discussing the development of experimental neuroses, suggested that certain experiences could create conditioned physiological and psychological responses in animals and humans, even though they occurred only once. Often these experiences were so dramatic that they created a cortical overload. That is, they generated so much arousal in the person that they overloaded the brain's ability to process information, leading to feelings of panic and confusion and eventually "turning off" the brain. In effect, the brain short-circuits and shuts down. When the individual comes to, he or she is confused, disoriented, and hypersuggestible; and his or her normal behavior patterns or habits might be disturbed for long periods of time. To illustrate this, Pavlov described the behavior of some laboratory animals in response to the Leningrad floods (Sargent, 1957).

The laboratory in which the animals were housed became flooded. The water came in under the door and began to fill the room. By the time someone was able to get into the room, it was already half-filled with water. The animals had been trapped in cages, unable to escape. The experience was so traumatic that many of the animals had severe behavioral disturbances which lasted for days and weeks afterwards.

Some months later, someone spilled water in the hall outside the laboratory door. Once again, water started to come under the laboratory door. As soon as the animals saw it, many of them reverted to the same neurotic behaviors that had developed following the flood. A simple cue had become significant enough to activate all of the natural pathways that the flood experience had opened up (Sargent, 1957).

It is quite likely that the animal experiences are good analogues for the flashback experiences that individuals have after they have taken a drug like LSD or experienced trauma in combat or on the athletic field. In fact, the brain's ability to do this might account for the effectiveness of catharsis experiences, which differ from flashbacks in that they are highly controlled immersions.

With catharsis, the intent is to recreate the experience. The individual can prepare in advance, and someone is always there to help him or her exert control during the experience and to reintegrate what has happened. This second person redirects the individual's attention to external cues when necessary to reestablish control.

As an individual becomes immersed in an experience, he or she recreates the connections between those neurons in the brain that are responsible for the original perceptions and feelings. A common example is when a person suddenly smells something that immediately transports him or her to grandmother's kitchen, or the lunchroom in the first grade. In the most extreme cases, the individual will recreate the body's original response, in the absence of any real environmental stimulus—he or she will see, taste, feel, and react to things that aren't there.

An example of this is the phenomena that have been reported during recreations of child abuse. Reliable therapists have reported seeing actual physiological changes in clients who were recreating abuse experiences. During an interview, a female therapist asked her client to describe the abuse that occurred. The client began to remember, and before long she was actually reliving the experience. By watching her client's eyes and posture and listening to her tone of voice, the therapist could tell that the woman was immersed. In becoming immersed, the client stopped shifting attention externally. On other occasions, this same therapist had clients interrupt their recall with a startled "I've been hit." The recreations were so vivid that their bodies actually responded as if they had been hit. Blood flowed to the area, redness occurred, and bruises developed.

At the beginning of this section I suggested that I might be stretching things by using immersion to explain mental alterations. In fact, we haven't located the structures in the brain, or the specific connections, that link thoughts with neural transmission and alterations in blood flow and glandular functions. However, it is likely that an explanation along these lines will eventually explain the changes some coaches have noted in athletes who have responded to hypnotic suggestions to reduce the pain associated with injury and to speed healing.

Body Image Change

People who have experienced ASCs claim that it seemed as if they were watching someone else performing their activities. A separation of mind and body seems to occur. An extreme example of this is out-of-body experiences, during which individuals claim that their spirits left their bodies. For the athlete, this separation of mind and body means that he or she can participate in sport without having to consciously process information. Somehow, the body engages in one set of activities while the mind engages in another.

What the athlete experiences in an altered state is similar to how you feel when you drive a car from one place to another and don't remember having driven because you were so caught up in your thoughts. The action, like the athlete's performance, has become a series of automatic responses. You react to cues like cars changing lanes, making turns, and stopping at stop signs without consciously thinking about them. Your brain, operating like radar, is prepared to take conscious control should the unexpected occur (e.g., the person in the car in front of you suddenly slams on the brakes).

This does not mean that your mind stops processing information while you are driving or playing in the zone. Rather, the processing that occurs is automatic, as opposed to the conscious, analytical thinking we use to solve problems. With training and experience, many of our responses become automatic, enabling us to react almost instinctively to stimuli. In the driving example, if you reacted to the situation of a suddenly stopping car by stepping on the brakes, you would probably continue attending to your internal focus without significant (or conscious) interruption. The flow of your thinking and behavior has been maintained.

When you can process and react to external information without conscious thought, you can perform two tasks at the same time. Your body automatically engages in a physical performance while your mind performs some other activity. Your body responds to the environment in spite of the fact that you are mentally immersed in your own thought processes. Often the internal immersion that occurs when driving on automatic results in a seemingly rapid passage of time. Your thoughts seem more intense and profound. You feel excited, and this enthusiasm keeps you focused internally. During all of this, external time seems to pass quickly. You arrive home from the drive before you realize it.

When athletes experience this, their minds are free to examine every aspect of the performance because they don't have to concentrate on what their bodies are doing. They can take in the entire atmosphere, watching the crowd and paying attention to the sights and sounds around them, without any interference. This would not be possible if they had not developed reflexive skills. This process of immersion will only be interfered with by a dramatic, unexpected occurrence such as the injury of another player, or a time-out that stops the action and forces you to begin thinking and analyzing.

A change in body image isn't always a positive experience. Some athletes have reported that they weren't able to feel what their bodies were doing. They became so caught up in a particular train of thought that any normal kinesthetic feedback was inhibited. When this happens, arousal levels get so high and attention becomes so narrowly focused that other signals can't get through.

Consider the example of Dan Jansen, a U.S. speed skater during the 1988 Olympics. Just prior to competition, this individual experienced a major tragedy in his life. He became so focused on competing for a family member who had passed away that he lost body awareness. He was skating extremely well and if nothing unexpected had happened he likely would have won an Olympic gold medal. Unfortunately, he stumbled and couldn't recover his balance because of his loss of awareness of his body. When he was asked what happened after the race he couldn't answer because he didn't know.

Hypersuggestibility

Hypersuggestibility is a state in which an individual is more responsive to suggestions than normal, as when a person is hypnotized. Although hypersuggestibility is not often associated with having a peak experience in sport or playing in the zone, it does occur in other kinds of ASC experiences. Playing in the zone doesn't usually increase suggestibility, but responsivity to suggestion is important to you for other reasons. For example, responsivity to suggestions can be an important means of inducing an ASC.

One of the ways we attempt to induce an ASC in athletes is through hypnosis or self-hypnosis. Your ability to develop a deep state of hypnosis depends upon your responsivity to suggestions, and the key elements to this responsivity are trust and willingness to cooperate. Without these elements, you will have trouble becoming immersed, breaking down the attentional shifting that occurs, and focusing attention on a coherent set of cues. If you don't trust yourself or the hypnotist, you will evaluate the process instead of responding to suggestions. You attend to the suggestion only long enough to debate whether you want to respond. That internal debate distracts you from the experience and encourages the shifting of attention that prevents the type of concentration leading to immersion.

The Dimensions of Consciousness

Figure 3.2 summarizes the importance of immersion in both achieving a peak performance and choking. Note the four different attentional focuses discussed in chapter 2. The square in the middle represents normal consciousness. Normal consciousness is what you experience during an average performance, when the constant shifting back and forth from an external to an internal focus prevents immersion from occurring. When shifting begins to break down, however, your involvement in one particular focus of attention becomes more complete (i.e., outside of your normal or typical experience).

Two different types of peak performance experiences can occur when you become immersed in an external focus of attention. If attention is narrowed and the number of cues you attend to is

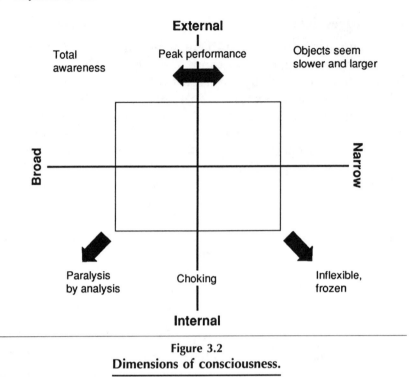

Figure 3.2
Dimensions of consciousness.

reduced (e.g., attending to the ball only), then your perception that things are happening more slowly and that objects are bigger will be enhanced. If your focus of attention is broader (e.g., taking in the whole playing field or tennis court), then that feeling of complete awareness—knowing what will happen before it occurs and being aware of the crowd—is emphasized.

When you play in the zone for any length of time, the width of your focus of attention will naturally shift (indicated by the two-headed arrow at the top of Figure 3.2) from a broad-external to a narrow-external focus. In tennis, for example, as the ball crosses to your opponent's side of the net, you have a broad focus and are aware of everything. This broad focus allows you to anticipate, move into position early, set up, and keep from feeling rushed. As the ball comes back and crosses to your side of the net, your concentration narrows. The ball seems to be slower and larger than normal. You feel in complete control, as if you could do anything you wanted. As soon as your racquet contacts the ball (not before), your attention automatically broadens. Absent is the shifting of attention to internal thoughts and feelings you have when reminding yourself to "bend" or "take the ball in front."

Now, consider what happens when you become internally immersed. It is this internal immersion that leads to choking in sports. As with an external focus, your attention can be either broad or narrow.

When your focus of concentration is narrow, your behavior is rigid or frozen (see the arrow in the bottom right-hand quadrant of Figure 3.2). Attentional shifting breaks down. You fail to attend to task-relevant external cues, and you are unable to think analytically. Instead, your thoughts are negative and self-defeating. To an outside observer, you look as if you were either not reacting at all, or repeating the same mistake without being able to adjust.

With a broad-internal focus of attention, you are more likely to appear scattered and flustered. You jump from one way of playing to another without being able to stick to anything. You might turn to problem solving (i.e., "paralysis by analysis") to improve your performance, or you might become immersed in feelings of fear, panic, frustration, or anger. In any case, your thoughts and feelings are distracting you, keeping you from reacting in an organized way to task-relevant environmental cues. Under these conditions, you feel rushed, overloaded, and pressured.

The Consciousness Continuum

Consciousness and the ability to concentrate lie on a continuum, with perfect task-relevant concentration at one end, and task-irrelevant concentration at the other. If you want to learn to minimize choking and maximize playing in the zone, you must learn to move along the consciousness continuum. (You never reach the end point in either direction.)

Playing in the zone does not represent the upper limits of your potential.

Another way to think of this is in terms of degrees of time distortion. When you have a peak performance, time seems to slow down to the point where you think you have reached perfection but you haven't. You have simply reached your "next level." As you learn to control attentional shifting you develop the skills that enable you to control movement along the consciousness continuum.

We all move along this consciousness continuum as we develop greater physical skill, regardless of whether we are actually working to develop our concentration skills. Increased physical skill decreases internal distractions. As your performance improves, the kinesthetic, visual, and auditory feedback cues that tell you something is wrong and that you need to correct it diminish. This gives you the sense that you have more time, because, without the distractions, you are shifting attention less and attending more to the environment.

Consider what happens when Greg Louganis performs an extremely complicated dive like a reverse three-and-one-half somersault off the 10-meter tower. His normal procedure is to spot the dive, that is, to briefly look back toward the tower to see where he is, and to use this information to time his opening. Greg is spinning at great speed, yet if you posted a paper with a five-digit number on it on the tower, he could tell you what the number was after the dive. Greg's ability to see the number is a reflection of his level of skill. To anyone else, seeing that number while diving off the 10-meter tower would indicate an altered state. But Greg has such a high level of skill that simply reading the number no longer represents an altered state. This has become his normal level of consciousness during a dive.

It is extremely important to think of consciousness as being on a continuum. If you don't, your tendency will be to search for perfection. You will expect to be in an altered state 100 percent of the time and that is never going to happen. It is the search for perfection, and the mistaken belief that they can obtain it, that keeps many athletes running from one miracle program to another. To help you get a better feeling for the consciousness continuum, let me describe the kind of shifting that goes on when the same athlete is seen as choking, playing normally, and playing in the zone.

Choking

A professional tennis player has had a series of poor performances. Janet has been struggling with her serve for some time and as a result has lost confidence in it. During several previous matches she has lost control of her serve at critical times. In spite of an inconsistent serve, Janet has done very well in doubles in the past. More recently, however, the doubles matches haven't gone that well either. Janet's doubles partner has had difficulty with her return of serve and has started missing volleys that she doesn't normally miss. In addition, Janet's partner seems to have lost confidence in her, expecting her serve to break down at critical moments. To further complicate things, communication has broken down between Janet and her coach. She feels that her coach is no longer supportive, instead criticizing her frequently. They have argued over how she should handle her current problems. She wants to please him, but she doesn't think that he understands her problems.

Janet and her partner have a first-round match against a team that they should be able to beat easily. The morning of the match she isn't feeling well. She is tired from staying up late the night before, and she is just about to start menstruating. This makes her feel sluggish and bloated. In addition, she has stomach cramps and is more emotionally reactive than normal.

In the first set, Janet struggles with these physical distractions. Under normal circumstances, such distractions would come and go, posing no serious problem. A confident player would be able to break away from these distractions and get back into the game.

In this match, however, Janet doesn't seem to be able to break away. In addition to her physical concerns, Janet is troubled by external (task-irrelevant) factors. She notices the game score as she is serving at 3-4 in the first set. She misses a first serve, hitting it into the bottom of the net—a sure sign that she is tight. She sees her partner looking at her. All of these things remind Janet of her serve problems. She starts to think negative thoughts and doubt herself. Her negative thoughts literally cause her muscles to tighten up. She double-faults when she can't generate enough racquet-head speed to hit a ball that she tossed too low.

Janet now becomes even more confused and overloaded. She starts to worry about her partner's errors in returning serve, which places more pressure on her to play well. She worries about what her coach thinks about the serve game she just lost. Controlled shifting of attention has broken down, and she is spending more and more time being internally focused, when she really needs to be able to watch the ball. At this point, Janet is experiencing an altered state. She feels rushed and unprepared, she can't see the ball, and she doesn't know what to do. She is overloaded by her physical state, her emotions, and her thoughts.

Normal Consciousness

Now, take that same player in a more normal situation. It could be the same doubles match, only 3 weeks later. Janet has been working on her serve and feels a bit more confident about it. She and her partner have had a couple of wins in which they played fairly well. She is a little tired, but she knows that's normal and doesn't worry about it. Things have been going well with her coach. Lately, they have been agreeing on what should be done. She has scouted the other team and knows their weaknesses. She is feeling fairly confident.

The match starts, and Janet and her partner win the toss and serve first. The teams stay on serve through 3-3, and it is her serve. She wins the first two points and is up 30-love. Then, she double-faults. She starts to get a little shaky, but several things happen. She looks at her coach and he doesn't seem too concerned. Her partner walks up to her and says, "No problem," and Janet senses that she is sincere. Janet reminds herself of the work she has been doing and feels reasonably confident that she can get her serve in, in spite of the tightness she feels. She makes a decision to play within the range of her abilities and not to go for too much; she knows that she doesn't have to be that good against this team.

Notice that this situation also involves internal distractions. Janet is not playing in the zone. She is, however, playing sound tennis. When distractions occur, they last for only a brief period of time. Her focus is shifting appropriately as she makes needed adjustments. In contrast to her earlier experience, Janet has managed to cope more effectively because she has more reasonable goals and isn't under as many pressures.

Playing in the Zone

In the first example, Janet's expectations were too high given the situation and her physical and emotional condition. Unfortunately, she was unable to lower those expectations. As a result, any sign that she wasn't performing well, or that the outcome of the match was in jeopardy made her more anxious and internally focused.

In the second situation, Janet was able to reduce her anxiety because she was able to establish and accept some more reasonable goals. She didn't have to serve perfectly. She knew she wasn't playing in the zone, but she wasn't going to choke, either! She was playing well enough to win.

Now, let's consider what happens when this athlete is playing in the zone. Janet has been playing well lately. She has just started working with a new coach, and the relationship is going really well. She selected the coach because he was understanding and supportive, and because he believed in her. She thinks her doubles partner is a fantastic player and is confident that even if she herself plays poorly, her partner is skilled enough to lift the entire team. She is not, however, worried about playing poorly—she has been playing very well.

Physically, Janet is strong and fit. In spite of the hard work she has been doing to get ready for the tournament, she is mentally and physically rested and ready to go. She enters the match feeling great and confident in herself, her coach, and her partner. Under these conditions, she really enjoys the tennis. Even when Janet makes a mistake, it has no negative, carryover effect on her concentration. She doesn't worry about correcting it, instead chalking it up to bad luck and nothing else. Almost all of the normal internal distractions that would prevent a person from becoming externally immersed are absent. As a result, Janet becomes totally caught up in the tennis, enters the zone, and plays out of her mind.

The only unfortunate aspect of this experience is that it occurred by chance rather than by design. Janet was fortunate: She was healthy, and she had both a new coach and new partner she could believe in. Had she worked to develop her concentration skills and to quiet distractions, she could count on becoming immersed even under more difficult situations.

Summary

The shifting of your attention back and forth from an external focus to an internal focus is one of the key factors in allowing you to judge the passage of time. Any breakdown in this shifting results in a dramatic change in your normal state of awareness.

The experience of playing in the zone tends to occur when an athlete's focus of attention is almost exclusively external. Performance is so automatic that there is very little need to shift to an internal focus of attention in order to analyze, make adjustments, and so on. Because the athlete is making fewer shifts, attention stays focused on task-relevant cues for longer periods of time. This can result in alterations in awareness. Time seems slowed down, objects are bigger and move more slowly. There is a feeling of complete control and the athlete seems to know what is going to happen even before it occurs.

The experience of choking occurs when attention becomes focused internally, and the athlete loses his or her ability to shift to an external focus and attend to performance-relevant cues. With less attention being paid to the ball or the opponent, time seems speeded up and the athlete feels pressured. Objects aren't as clear and the ability to anticipate decreases dramatically.

The solution to choking, and the key to playing in the zone, is simple. Control your shifting of attention. Find ways of staying out of your head. To accomplish this, you will have to be sensitive to distractions and to have specific strategies for breaking away from them and refocusing attention. Most important, you will have to make a commitment to the program. You will have to practice breaking away and refocusing!

A key to making a significant change in your own performance is being sensitive to subtle changes in your awareness. Learn, for example, to be sensitive to those performance situations that seem to cause time to speed up. Be able to identify the differences between your thoughts and feelings in those situations where time is slowed down versus those where it is speeded up. Learn to identify the people or performance situations that seem to cause you to become too emotional.

CHAPTER 4

THE IMPORTANCE OF FAITH IN YOUR MENTAL AND PHYSICAL ABILITIES

Faith exists on a continuum. Learning to play in the zone means learning how to be comfortable with occasional doubts and unsure outcomes.

The previous chapters underlined the importance of becoming immersed and playing in the zone. Controlling attention and shifting concentration from an external to an internal focus are essential to this process. The ability to control concentration, however, is as much an art as it is a science. Your willingness to trust yourself, develop faith in your abilities, and believe in the ideas presented in this book is critical to learning to play in the zone.

Learning to play in the zone requires you to develop a strong set of beliefs and to deepen your faith in yourself and your mental abilities.

It's not hard to temporarily change your perceptions to get you to play better. Anything you do to reduce the number of internal distractions you experience will result in more effective concentration. When you concentrate more effectively you begin to move along the consciousness continuum toward external immersion.

Unfortunately, unless you take responsibility for reducing the distractions you normally experience, any changes that occur will be short-lived. For example, getting a new tennis partner may temporarily reduce the distractions that were associated with a lack of confidence in your old partner. The more you play together, however, the more you learn about each other's weaknesses. Your doubts return, but you still haven't learned how to get rid of them (other than continually shifting partners, coaches, etc.).

By manipulating the environment and searching for temporary solutions (e.g., a new putter or a new shoe), you avoid learning how to gain control over concentration. You may have moments when you feel confident and even think you have faith in yourself, but these feelings don't last. Your self-confidence and faith are both extremely shallow. If things go well, you perform well. If things do not go well, negative thoughts take over and you lose control. You haven't learned to stop the negative thinking by focusing on the positive. You haven't developed the faith you need to make do with what you have.

Faith is important because it quiets the voice of doubt inside your head. Unless you quiet self-doubt, you cannot become immersed.

In chapter 3 I described what happened to a tennis player in three different situations. When Janet choked, her faith broke down. She no longer believed in her serve, her partner, her coach, the things she had been working on, or the things she was being told to do during the match. She was tormented by doubts and unable to stay focused on the environment. In essence, she had no confidence in her ability to be successful.

When Janet played in the zone, it was clear that she felt self-confident. She had worked hard to improve her fitness and technique, and that helped remove her doubts. Fortunately, many things happened to be going well for Janet (e.g., her partner was playing well), because she really hadn't worked on developing the concentration skills that would help her in the long run. Such skills are necessary for recovering from negative thinking, which arises when performance problems inevitably occur.

The Difference Between Belief and Faith

Believing in something and having self-confidence are not the same as having the kind of faith that allows you to stop self-destructive thinking. It is possible to believe in something without having much faith in it. The differences will become clear in the next sections.

Seeing Is Believing

Most of us believe in something. The strength of our beliefs, however, tends to be directly related to performance or outcome. If we succeed, our beliefs are reinforced. Boris Becker believes in his serve; John Bertrand, skipper of the Australia II (the yacht that won the Americas Cup in 1983) believed in his crew; and Larry Bird believes in his ability to make a basket under pressure. These beliefs will remain strong as long as the individuals who hold them continue to be successful. However, because beliefs are based on external factors, they are changeable. If the object of the belief no longer brings success, then the individual will begin to question and/or modify his or her belief.

Although beliefs often change, a belief or a set of beliefs is a prerequisite to developing faith. You can believe without having faith, but you cannot have faith without also believing. A belief is simply a position statement. Beliefs do not have to carry any commitment to action; that is, they don't necessarily influence behavior. For example, if I say "I believe in the democratic party," I mean that I agree with the philosophy that underlies that particular political party. This doesn't mean that I will always vote democrat. Why? Because in spite of my belief, I have little faith in the likelihood that the party (or individuals in it) will behave according to their philosophy.

Belief in your abilities is closely tied to self-confidence. Self-confidence comes from both hard work and success. Your self-confidence is higher when you know you have put in the work and are prepared. That preparation goes a long way toward helping you reduce the negative thoughts that interfere with performance.

The difference between belief and faith can be seen in the performance of the Oakland A's in the 1988 and 1989 World Series. The A's had a great deal of confidence in their ability to win the 1988 World Series. They believed that they were a much stronger team than the Los Angeles Dodgers. This belief was confirmed by others, at least on paper. But when a Dodger player hit a game-winning home run in the ninth inning of the first game, the team's spirit and belief in its ability seemed to die. The A's never recovered from that first game loss, and though they believed in their ability to win, they lacked faith.

The A's experience in 1988 can be contrasted with their preparation for 1989. Through the 1989 season the A's worked to develop faith in the belief that they would win the World Series. They identified all of their strengths, all of the reasons they were the better team and focused on these. Through the development of faith, their belief became unshakable.

In 1988 the A's had not worked to develop faith in their beliefs. Under pressure in the World Series they couldn't keep negative thoughts from interfering with performance. That same thing happens to the individual athlete who goes into a game believing that he or she is prepared and finds the other person playing better than expected. This experience undermines the player's self-confidence. The athlete begins to believe that he or she isn't really that good and as a result, plays well below his or her potential.

Consider the plight of Ivan Lendl in the quarterfinals of the French Open in 1989. He was playing 17-year-old Michael Chang. Lendl won the first two sets easily. Then, for some reason he got a little tight; instead of going for winners, he just kept the ball in play. Chang rallied and evened the match at two sets a piece.

In the third set, Chang was exhausted and suffering from cramps, which were so bad at times, he couldn't stretch to serve the ball. He was hitting underhanded serves and floating "moon balls" to give himself time to recover and get back into points.

By this time, Lendl's confidence had deteriorated to the point where he could not take advantage of Chang. The match ended on Lendl's serve, when he double-faulted at match point for

Chang. Lendl's problems were mental. He had become tentative, playing not to lose, instead of to win. Chang played tough, and when he did, Lendl began to doubt himself and lose confidence. He essentially lost a match that shouldn't have been close!

Faith Is Believing in the Absence of Success

We all lose confidence from time to time. Faith differs from beliefs and self-confidence in that it isn't dependent upon outcome and success. Faith involves continuing to play as if you are going to win, even when all the evidence is against it. John Paul Jones had it when his ship was sinking and he told the English, "Surrender. I have just begun to fight." Faith has to be developed—it isn't something you are born with.

When Chris Evert lost 11 straight matches to Martina Navratilova, yet continued to believe she would win the next one, she demonstrated faith. She continued to believe that she was making important progress, in spite of the fact that behavior (as reflected by the outcome of the match) didn't reflect that. Evert's faith allowed her to maintain a commitment that very few athletes match.

Deeply religious individuals believe that God is a loving, caring, involved creator who plays an active role in their lives and that He responds to prayer. They hold on to and act on that belief (by praying and continuing to behave as if God loved them and cared for them) even when everything around them says it isn't true. These people have faith that goes beyond believing and supports them when things aren't going so well.

Many athletes believe in their ultimate potential, but very few have the faith that allows them to set aside negative thinking when things aren't going according to plan. Most athletes lack the faith that quiets the inner voice of doubt. Those who do have it are able to say "I don't know how, but I know it will work out." Steffi Graf has such faith in her forehand—one that says "No matter what, I must go for my shot." Most athletes believe and will tell you that they have to go for their shot when they are in a winning position. At the same time, unlike Steffi, most of them will tighten up and play conservatively. They believe, but they lack the faith that allows them to act in accordance with their belief.

Roadblocks to the Development of Faith

You must learn to develop the kind of faith described in the previous section if you want to calm the fears and doubts that cause you to choke and keep you from reaching your full potential. Two roadblocks make it difficult, but not impossible, to develop faith. Understanding how to overcome them is the first step to finding the source of strength that exists inside you to have faith in your abilities.

You Can't Expect Miracles

In chapter 3 I indicated that a spontaneous experience of a peak performance or playing in the zone is negative as well as positive. It's a great feeling, but because it happens spontaneously, without any systematic preparation, you can't count on its happening again. Let's look at this process more closely.

Imagine that you suddenly find yourself playing better than you ever dreamed you could. It feels like someone suddenly turned on a switch, as you find yourself performing at higher and higher levels. More often than not, you come away from those experiences feeling that if you could just find the right magic word, thought, or position, you could flip on that switch whenever you wanted to. It doesn't occur to you that playing in the zone on a regular basis is a matter of self-discipline, a skill that needs to be developed through faithful adherence to a set of procedures. After all, you didn't work to experience it the first time; in fact, everything seemed so easy! Why should you have to work now?

Unfortunately, that myth is perpetuated by individuals who want to sell books and tapes designed to give quick solutions to difficult problems. When people find themselves playing in the zone, they are really motivated to discover the secret to help them do it at will. There is a market out there—athletes are willing to pay to play better. Sharp business people are quick to realize that the promise of a miracle will sell to a person who is hungry for one!

Any bookstore in the U.S. offers a wide range of books promising to enhance performance. Some of these offer excellent suggestions that would be very useful if adhered to faithfully.

Unfortunately, when the suggestions don't result in an immediate transformation, most athletes simply figure they've grabbed the wrong book. They drop that book and grab the next one that comes along.

This doesn't mean that athletes are lazy. Instead, they really want to believe that a miracle can change their performance. Things should click, and when they don't, athletes blame the material, rather than seeing the real cause of the problem—their own lack of faith. We need to stop looking for miracles and recognize that performance will always be variable. The baseball pitcher won't always pitch a perfect game, the hitter won't bat a thousand, the tennis player won't win every match, and the golfer won't par every hole.

Faith Is Not Absolute

The block to faith is the belief that you either have faith or you don't. Even extremely religious people question their faith in God, because they don't feel God's presence all the time. They expect to feel filled with the Holy Spirit 24 hours a day, and when they don't, they think something is wrong.

The misconception of absolute faith is tied closely to the tendency to expect miracles. This is true in both sport and religion. For example, a young man, without a great deal of preparation, suddenly experiences a religious conversion. He goes to a revival meeting with a friend and suddenly finds himself immersed in a religious experience. This is similar to a peak performance in sport, except that the content is religious and the focus is on God. He is overwhelmed and, for the moment, feels fulfilled. At this moment, his faith seems absolute; however, as he moves away from the experience his faith weakens and he begins to have doubts. This person failed to realize that continued faith requires commitment in the face of doubt, and that commitment is something he has to provide for himself.

The same thing happens with athletes, who seem to experience miracles daily. Say one particular baseball player has a bad game, batting 0-4 and not making contact with the ball. After the game, he immediately starts searching for a quick fix. He heads for the batting cage and starts experimenting with his swing. It isn't long before something seems to click and he starts hitting the cover off the ball. He comes running out of the batting cage saying "I've solved my problem! I wasn't digging in quite deep enough at the plate" and "I just realized that I haven't been wrapping my bat enough."

This athlete is absolutely convinced that he has found a miracle—a technical solution or key that is going to make him hit 400. He doesn't bother to remember that he was practicing under nonstressful conditions. He fails to recognize that his swing was interfered with by excess muscle tension as well as his inability to focus concentration on the ball under pressure. By finding a miracle, this player hasn't done anything to make the changes he needs to make. He hasn't developed faith in a procedure that will allow him to clear his mind of the self-doubts and negative thoughts that increase tension in pressure situations. What he has done by finding a miracle is temporarily reducing the anxiety that occurs when he fails. Unfortunately, this temporary reduction in anxiety prevents long-term positive change.

Chances are, if I were to suggest that this person hadn't found a solution, that he was fooling himself, and that his faith in the solution to his problem was extremely shallow, he would probably say that I was undermining his self-confidence. *Athletes like this are afraid of being afraid.* They have not learned to be comfortable with doubts, or with the knowledge that they don't have all the answers. Faith isn't something either we have, or we don't. It exists on a continuum, which leaves room for occasional self-doubt. Learning to become immersed and play in the zone means learning how to be comfortable with occasional doubts and unsure outcomes. You have to recognize that you can perform well without having all the answers. Faith is a matter of degree, and you must work to deepen it.

Faith is not an all-or-none concept. Everyone has doubts from time to time. In fact, it is within the context of those doubts that you measure the depth of your faith. The greater the doubts and the more faithful your adherence to your beliefs, the deeper your faith. You can only grow and develop faith when you are challenged by doubts and adversity.

You Develop Faith by Making a Commitment

Individuals who have disciplined and prepared themselves for peak performances in sport benefit beyond the immediate situation. They recognize that their experiences are high points that they have earned. They realize that they won't play in the zone 24 hours a day. There will be times of doubt, but these athletes know that they have the power to do something about that doubt. Truly great athletes realize they have a responsibility to develop their talents. This involves making a commitment and honoring it so that they can grow. Doubts are seen as a part of life, not as excuses to stop training or working. In sport, this type of commitment is essential to achieving your full potential. You can't look for miracles—you can't expect God, a coach, a piece of equipment, or a chemical to do it for you.

You have the capacity to believe and to have faith in your own abilities. It is your responsibility, however, to develop that faith by making a commitment.

Disciplined and committed individuals are able to exert incredible control over their feelings and abilities. A few years ago in the World University Games, a young Russian diver hit his head on the tower while he was attempting a reverse three-and-one-half somersault. The diver was killed, and the competition was held up for over 30 minutes to clear the blood from the water. The diver who was to follow the young Russian was Greg Louganis. As it happened, Louganis had elected to attempt the same dive as the Russian. His sense of control and faith in his own ability enabled him to successfully complete the dive. If Greg had doubts at that time, his faith and level of commitment allowed him to set those doubts aside and get on with the task at hand.

Greg provided yet another example of this faith in the 1988 Olympics in Seoul. On his 9th dive in the preliminary competition of the 3-meter event, he hit his head on the diving board. He was attempting a reverse two-and-one-half somersault in pike position. After receiving several stitches in his head, he managed to complete his 10th and 11th dives and to make it into the finals on the following day. During the finals he had to execute a near-perfect reverse two-and-one-half somersault to stay in the running for a gold medal. He did, and he won the gold medal on his 11th dive by performing a reverse three-and-one-half somersault.

Looking at videotapes of Greg just before he begins his approach for the reverse two-and-one-half somersault in the Olympic finals, it's apparent that he has concerns, and possibly doubts, about this dive. You can see it in his face and in the relief that he shows after the dive is over. Because he is human, Greg had doubts. Because he had trained so hard and because he had developed faith, Greg was able to set the doubts aside long enough to perform.

Summary

Having faith means accepting responsibility. Learning to play in the zone requires discipline and hard work. Discipline builds faith in those things that will quiet the voices of doubt, but these voices will resist being controlled. Your greatest battle won't be outside, in the competitive environment, but inside your mind.

Faith and your ability to play in the zone grow slowly, hand in hand.

If you already have the self-discipline required to make a commitment to a training program, then the only thing keeping you from developing faith is your fear of failure and rejection. This fear causes you to look for a quick solution rather than a long-term program for improving performance.

CHAPTER 5

HOW TO DEVELOP FAITH AND OVERCOME SELF-DOUBT

**Press ahead with your program in spite of doubts.
Deep faith leads you to make a real commitment,
which leads to the development of a deeper faith.**

To achieve your full potential, you must develop faith in both your ability to accept responsibility and solve problems and in the procedures you intend to use. This is not an easy task. Fortunately, we all have the abilities and equipment necessary to develop confidence and control concentration—but it's up to each of us to make the most of these skills. The athlete who believes in a coach, a training program, or a piece of equipment, but doesn't accept responsibility for developing faith in that belief, won't be able to follow through on his or her program when doubts occur. The athlete must develop methods for redirecting concentration in the face of doubts and make a commitment to follow through in spite of the doubts.

Responsibility for your life rests in your own hands.

You first must develop faith that the responsibility is yours. Your challenge is to take responsibility for developing your abilities and making the most out of your life. Others may offer support and make suggestions regarding specific beliefs you should adhere to, but ultimately it is your decision. It is not enough to say yes today, and we'll see about tomorrow. To develop your full potential, you must find some beliefs (principles, techniques, etc.) that you can adhere to, to the point of developing faith in them. You must stick with your decision, no matter how many doubts occur.

You will continue to look for miracles until you accept responsibility for your own behavior.

Once you accept responsibility for your own behavior, you stop looking for miracles and are in a position to make a commitment to achieving your full potential. As soon as you stop looking for miracles, however, you immediately have doubts about your skill, knowledge, and ability to make critical decisions.

Striving for Perfection Is Okay, But Expecting Perfection Can Be Crippling

Many athletes have difficulty accepting responsibility for their behaviors because they believe they have to be perfect. Such individuals will always fall short of their goals and, as a result, never develop the self-confidence it takes to make the commitment to work hard to reach their potentials.

In a recent newspaper article, a father indicated that neither he nor his wife put any pressure on their son. And in direct evidence against this, he then told the reporter that both he and his wife had sacrificed good jobs and were spending $25,000 per year on their son's training to give him every advantage. In the same article the son was quoted as saying, "My parents don't put any pressure on me, they just want me to be happy. How can I let them down when they have done so much for me?"

That young man is headed for self-destruction. He denies that he feels any pressure, and he has come to accept the idea that anything less than perfection means failure. This is typical of athletes in situations where everything seems to depend on the bottom line—whether they win or lose. These individuals deny they feel pressured to be perfect, while their behavior clearly reveals that they can't accept anything less. They scream and yell, throw tantrums, and become depressed when things don't go right.

It's impossible to accept responsibility for your behavior if you feel you have to be perfect. Failing to live up to unrealistic expectations destroys confidence and feelings of self-worth. To avoid those feelings, many athletes make excuses for their problems, blaming bad luck, bad officiating, bad coaching, and the like.

Perfectionism Leads to Internal Distractions

Human beings react to the pressure to be perfect in one of two ways: They become angry and blame others for their failures, or they become convinced that they are no good. As pressure increases in competitive situations, the first individual becomes extremely sensitive to any cue that provides a focus (and an excuse) for her anger. She looks for things to blame for her own failure. Voices of anger inside her distract her from focusing on the game. Under these conditions, it is impossible to become immersed. The individual with self-doubts reacts to the pressure by telling himself he's no good. Instead of concentrating on the competition, he listens to the voice of self-doubt and ends up withdrawing and giving up.

It isn't easy to quiet these internal distractions. The need to be perfect drives a lot of athletes toward greatness. As long as they can cope with the pressure and the competition, they are fine. When they start to lose, however, it isn't long before that drive, which was once a strength, becomes a major liability.

Substitute Doing Your Best for Being Perfect

Overcoming those internal distractions is a major challenge, but you can take charge! You will have to work as hard at controlling your concentration as you had to work at developing your physical skills, but you can do it. You start by countering the irrational belief that you must be perfect. Then, you substitute a belief that provides you with support and direction and motivates you to play as well as you can, while allowing you to accept something less than perfection.

It isn't whether you win or lose, but how you play the game.

Believing this will provide you with the motivation you need, while relieving some of the pressure you feel. "How you play the game" means taking responsibility for your actions, even when you lose or don't play as well as you thought you could. As an athlete, you must learn to judge yourself on the basis of desire and intent, rather than success or failure.

The emphasis on the performance, as opposed to the outcome, doesn't mean that making the right decision or winning the contest isn't important. Obviously, the outcome is important. However, the only way to remove the fears and doubts that keep you from playing your best is to remove the pressure to be perfect. Once you have done this, the little voice inside your head that screams out in fear and panic when you lose a point, strike out, or make an error will begin to quiet down.

Anxiety about losing only increases the internal noise. Your belief that playing well is important will reduce your anxiety about losing and help you gain some control over one source of distraction. When losing is less of an issue, you can let go of doubts and past mistakes and keep them from affecting your performance.

If how you play the game is more important than whether you win or lose, then how are you to play the game?

Believe it is your responsibility to do the very best you can with the tools you have.

There will be days when the tools you have aren't going to be enough. Lots of things will work against you. You will be sick and tired, luck will go against you, and you'll get bad calls from officials. You'll have days when you are outmatched and outclassed. And sometimes things will go against you in spite of your best efforts. Finally, there will be days when the better player doesn't win. The only way to avoid aggravating these situations is to accept those things that are beyond your control and play to the best of your ability given the conditions of the day.

Consider the basketball team that has lost confidence in one of its teammates during a game on the basis of poor play. There may not be anything constructive to do about it, other than not allowing it to affect the play of other members of the team. They are trapped by circumstances that are beyond their control. Their task is to play as well as they can, independent of this particular individual. The players have two options. They can elevate their level of play to compensate for one player's weakness. However, if the pressure to compensate increases the team's voices of doubt and tension, everyone's performance will deteriorate. The players' other option is to forget about trying to compensate and simply play their own games.

Having faith in the conviction that it is not whether you win or lose, but how you play the game helps you cope with situations like this. There are times when you must accept some limitations. Believing this makes it easier to control the voices of doubt that cause you to give up or press too hard.

Accept the fact that faith is a growing process, not an absolute.

When your doubts become too strong, no matter how hard you have been working, and when the pressure to be perfect creeps back in, you must learn to accept that the strength of your faith will decrease. It is at these times that you must press ahead with your program, in spite of doubts. Growth involves taking two steps forward and one step backward. Remember, deep faith leads you to make a real commitment, and making a real commitment leads to the development of a deeper faith. You cannot have one without the other.

Develop Faith That You Can Play in the Zone

It's essential to develop faith in your ability to play in the zone. If you don't have faith that you can control your ability to play in the zone and avoid choking, you won't work at it! You develop this faith by quieting your inner voices of anger and self-doubt.

This is an important point to understand. Playing in the zone first requires a level of physical skill that enables you to perform without having to think about it. For example, when playing in the zone, the tennis player doesn't talk to herself about how to play the point, how to set up for a shot, or how to hit the ball.

When developing and learning new skills, you talk to yourself a great deal. You remind yourself of simple things: "Take your time, step up to the foul line, and take a deep breath. Bend your knees, and follow through." This self-talk helps you develop and grow, enabling you to make needed adjustments and corrections during the learning process. It reminds you to practice the same thing until it becomes automatic.

This self-talk is greatly diminished when you are playing in a game. At this point, you are attempting to use skills that are already developed. When you are in the zone, you don't have to think tactics because the appropriate move is obvious to you. Things like setting up and preparing early should happen automatically.

Use Conscious Reminders to Stay in the Zone

Once you reach the point where you play automatically, you can be assured that you are capable of entering the zone. If you have the physical skills to play automatically, but aren't playing in the zone, it's because you are having to think about things to make yourself work. For example, if you are physically tired, you might have to consciously motivate yourself to get to the ball.

Using conscious reminders helps you overcome certain limitations that make it difficult to enter or stay in the zone. A fatigued athlete who is failing to move and get into position has to constantly remind himself to move. He has to consciously work to get started, and that effort becomes an internal distraction. Likewise, an athlete that finds himself preoccupied with the outcome of a competition has to continually remind himself to let those thoughts go and pay attention to task-relevant cues. He must get out of his head! It is critical to learn what to attend to and what to say to yourself to get externally immersed, overcoming the interference you are struggling with.

Consciously attend to cues that reduce the inner voices.

If you are feeling confident, and if you know that the fatigue you are feeling is normal, then consciously making yourself work is going to improve your performance. If you are having a technical problem, and you are confident that you can fix it, then a quick reminder to make a certain correction will improve performance. In both of these examples, the internal distractions and the attentional shifts that occur will be brief. Following a minor adjustment, you will begin to become immersed in external cues.

This is not true when you lack confidence in yourself and your ability to solve problems. If you lack confidence, have doubts about the best technical or tactical move, or are choking, the key to improving your performance lies not in thinking about tactical or technical cues, which only adds to your inner voices, but in finding ways to get immersed in the competition. Without confidence you begin to question your own solutions, debating with yourself instead of concentrating on task-relevant cues like your opponent or your performance. To avoid this, you must learn to attend to triggers or simple cues that control a whole sequence of movements without any conscious thought on your part. The techniques presented in subsequent chapters were designed to get you immersed. *To use them effectively, you must build faith in them!*

The techniques of centering, self-hypnosis, attentional refocusing, and mental rehearsal that you use to quiet doubts are just tools, not magical solutions. Their continued success rests in your faithful use of them. Your task is simply to choose one of them and stick to it. You cannot quiet the voices inside you and enter the zone if you don't take a stand and build your faith in the method you choose. It's not worth agonizing over which to choose—there aren't that many differences among the psychological techniques available. If you aren't playing up to your potential, then which technique you choose isn't as important as simply deciding on one of them and working to build faith in your choice.

Use Criticism and Self-Doubt to Develop Faith

If you want to grow and develop as an athlete, you must be able to use criticism and self-doubt to your own advantage. Too many athletes react to criticism as a personal attack, a rejection, or a sign of failure. Actually, criticism and self-doubt challenge the athlete to grow and develop in his or her faith.

You cannot learn anything new from performance that you perceive to be perfect. You can only learn from mistakes. Your faith and commitment are strengthened when you are challenged and tested. You must develop faith in the belief that criticism and doubt are necessary for growth.

Conclusion

Negative beliefs contribute to the doubts that keep you from playing in the zone. By developing faith in the following positive beliefs, you can begin to overcome the voice of doubt.

1. Recognize that faith is neither an absolute feeling, nor a sense of confidence and peace that never leaves you. Even the most faithful have doubts.
2. Stop looking for a miracle that will give you freedom from doubt and anxiety, once and for all.
3. Recognize that developing faith and self-confidence is a growing process that happens over time, by disciplining yourself to adhere to beliefs and tools in the face of anxiety and doubt.
4. Take the responsibility for developing faith. You accomplish your goal by making choices about the tools you will use and the things you will believe in, and then making a commitment to those choices.
5. Develop faith in the belief that you can play in the zone.
6. Use criticism and doubt to build strength.

Summary

Think about the issues presented in this chapter. Developing confidence and faith depends upon making a commitment. You can strengthen your ability to make that commitment. The first thing you must do is build faith in the fact that you are responsible for what happens. Behave as if you believe that you are in control, whether you actually feel that way or not.

To do anything other than accept responsibility for your behavior is to make excuses, to blame others, and to create internal conflicts that destroy your ability to concentrate on the task. There will be times when everything around you suggests that you are out of control. These times will test your ability to play with confidence and the strength of your belief that you can take control. When Vince Lombardi told people the Green Bay Packers "didn't lose games, they ran out of time," he was demonstrating faith that they were in control. He held this belief in spite of the fact that the scoreboard indicated otherwise. Because he and the team held this belief, they won more games than others would have in similar situations. They won because their faith quieted internal distractions.

To develop faith in your ability to win and to become confident, play as if you are in control.

CHAPTER 6

DEVELOPING A CONCENTRATION SKILLS TRAINING PROGRAM

Our goal wasn't to change her swimming times. We wanted to develop her faith in the belief that her times would drop by helping her focus on the positive.

Chapter 1 listed the criteria to use in deciding whether your performance problems require a psychological intervention or a technical change. Making that diagnosis is the first step in improving concentration and committing yourself to a training program. As soon as you determine the nature of your problem, you reduce the number of issues that you have to deal with. Your feelings of confusion decrease as you gain a sense of direction and structure, and that makes it easier to think and to concentrate.

If you decide that your problem is psychological, the next step is to select an intervention technique. This involves finding a technique you can believe and build faith in.

Choosing the Right Technique: Two Examples

Several techniques are used to help athletes learn to concentrate, but most athletes develop their own favorites. They find something in the technique that feels comfortable, makes sense, and is consistent with their previous learning. This helps them develop faith in the procedures, which leads to a commitment to practice, and practice, in turn, increases faith.

The techniques presented in this book feel right to me. They fit with my own training background in the martial arts and are consistent with material I have studied about human perception, memory, and learning. I have used them myself and have helped others make good use of them.[1]

Both the sport psychologist and the athlete need to be able to see how the techniques can be directly applied to the problems they are trying to deal with. That means that the procedures need to make sense to them. The sport psychologist has to show the athlete how the techniques offer concrete, behavioral solutions to psychological problems. This is how the sport psychologist helps the athlete develop the necessary faith to follow through on and practice the procedures.

In choosing the right technique for a particular athlete, the sport psychologist and the athlete first must clearly define the problem. They identify the situation and exactly how it is affecting behavior, taking baseline measures of the mistakes that are occurring. They determine

- how frequently the problem occurs,
- how emotionally intense the problem is (i.e., how tight does the athlete get physically and how much control does he or she lose over muscle tension and/or focus of concentration), and
- how long the loss of control lasts.

Two examples from my own experience should show you how this is done. A pitcher playing AA ball and trying to move up told me that he had a problem with left-handed hitters. To help this individual, the first thing I had to do was determine if the

---

[1]I have written several books that detail a wide variety of psychological techniques. These include *The Inner Athlete*, available through Enhanced Performance Services, Oakland, CA, and *Athletes' Guide to Mental Training*, published by Human Kinetics.

problem was technical or psychological. One of the quickest ways to do that is to establish the history of his problem.

Talking with the pitcher, I learned that the problem had developed quite recently. In fact, he had never experienced any special difficulties pitching to left-handers until he got to this particular training camp. His problem seemed to have originated after he pitched for the first time during the camp. A coach whom he respected and knew would have some say in his career pointed out that he had struggled against left-handed hitters that day.

The athlete listened, but didn't let the comment affect him, or so he thought. He knew that he hadn't had problems before and concluded that it was just a bad day. Nevertheless, his confidence wasn't that high, especially under the pressure of being observed by the pitching coach. In fact, in the very next game, he became acutely aware of the fact that he was facing a left-hander in the first inning.

The little bit of history I collected indicated that the pitcher had the necessary technical skills to pitch to left-handers (he had done so for several previous seasons). His problem had developed relatively recently. The more we talked, the more we realized that the pressure he was feeling to perform was affecting him in two ways. First, he was beginning to tighten up in the neck and shoulders when he faced left-handers, and this was affecting his delivery. Second, his doubts were causing him to try to guide the ball instead of just reaching back and firing. In effect, his normal technique had been altered because of changes in both tension and his normal thinking process. The mechanical adjustments he had been trying to make weren't working because he was still pitching with too much tension and too many distractions. Under those conditions, it was impossible for him to maintain any type of consistency.

After talking with the pitcher, I asked him to throw a few pitches to a catcher without any batter in the batter's box. After he had thrown about 10 pitches, I asked him to throw to a particular spot (e.g., low and away). He moved the ball around, showing both of us that he had good control. Then I asked him if he had been actually looking at the spot he was pitching to (i.e., was he staring at the catcher's glove?). He realized that he wasn't; instead, he was getting his sign, seeing the position of the catcher, and then mentally throwing to a spot. Pitching was such an automatic response that he didn't have to stare at a target.

This particular athlete's concern over left-handers and what the coach was thinking resulted in his doing something that was unnatural for him. He was looking to a spot and trying to guide the ball. Once he recognized that, it was easy to convince him that we had to introduce a procedure that would help him control his negative thinking and excessive muscle tension.

Notice that I didn't just tell the athlete to learn to relax. First of all, he didn't need to relax when pitching to right-handers. Second, a general instruction like that makes no sense. He needed to be able to see why relaxation would help, and under what conditions. He needed a particular focus. Notice also that by providing a focus, I could tell whether the intervention we used was working. In this particular case, my goal was not to get the athlete to strike out the next left-handed hitter he faced, but to get him to return to his normal pitching motion, independent of the outcome. Neither the pitcher nor I had total control over the hitter. Left-handers were going to get some hits. Our immediate concern had to do with making sure the pitcher didn't help the hitter. We would judge the success of the program on the basis of the pitcher's throwing motion and feeling about his delivery.

Using self-hypnosis (chapter 9) and focusing on left-handed batters, this athlete was able to experience a dramatic change in his performance. Within 2 days, his normal motion returned, and he had no further problems during the remainder of the training camp. At last report he was doing well.

My second example concerns a 17-year-old female swimmer who was referred to me by her coach. According to the coach, this young woman had a lot of potential. Her training had been progressing nicely, and she was a sure candidate for a college scholarship (which was important to the athlete and her parents). The coach was concerned because she had lost confidence in herself and in the swimming program. Although she was continuing with the workouts, she was depressed and had told the coach that she was thinking of quitting swimming altogether.

At first, the problem seemed pretty global. It wasn't as nicely confined as the pitcher's problem in the previous example. Talking with the athlete, however, helped both of us realize that situational factors were playing a major role in the difficulties she was facing.

At the start of the season the coach had introduced a new training program. It consisted of heavy work that tears an athlete down and makes her very tired. They were training through less important meets to peak for the championships. As a result, this athlete had not even come close to her best times of the previous year. This had eroded her confidence in the program and in her ability. Her coach had told her that swimming times would drop, but this wasn't enough to convince her.

This swimmer's loss of self-confidence matched what I and Jeff Bond, chief sport psychologist at the Australian Institute for Sport, found earlier during a research project on over 2,000 athletes. We wanted to see what happens to self-esteem in male and female athletes between the ages of 13 and 25 (see Figure 6.1).

As you can see in Figure 6.1, girls around 13 have higher levels of self-confidence than boys of the same age. This relationship immediately begins to change: Male self-confidence increases until about 18 years of age, whereas female self-confidence

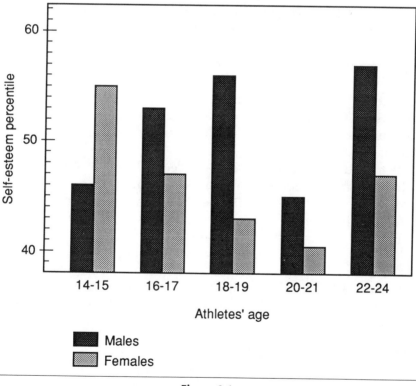

Figure 6.1
Self-esteem as a function of age.

actually decreases. Through this period, boys are rapidly gaining in strength, whereas girls' development slows down. This is because girls have matured earlier than boys and, in fact, can outperform them at age 13.

In swimming, where athletes work out together, it is common for them to compare changes in their own levels of performance with those of the other athletes in the program. When male swimmers continue to improve, even through extremely hard training cycles, some female swimmers expect to do the same, and that's when they lose their confidence.

Look at Figure 6.1 again. By the time athletes reach 18 years of age, both boys and girls are fairly well matured. They have reached a critical stage in their lives. They are about to leave high school and must make major decisions about the future. At this point, even male self-esteem drops, reflecting a period of self-doubt. Those men and women who overcome this and continue in their sports either recover from that temporary loss of self-esteem or never experienced it in the first place.

Using this information, I convinced this particular swimmer that her feelings weren't unique. She wasn't alone, and that knowledge helped to reduce the anxiety she was feeling about the things that were going on. She realized that her goals had been unreasonable and had contributed to her unhappiness and depression.

As a result of our discussion, we decided to use self-hypnosis to help her modify her negative thinking. Our goal was to increase both the number of her positive thoughts and her motivation for training. I emphasized that our goal wasn't to change her swimming times. Instead, we wanted to develop her faith in the belief that her times would drop by helping her focus on the positive and by placing her current depression in proper perspective. Happily, her attitude changed and her times did drop. In fact, they dropped even more than the coach had expected.

Making Conscious Practices Automatic

You need to be aware of one last area in which doubts can creep in as you attempt to learn to control concentration, avoid choking, and play in the zone.

In everyday life we sometimes encounter logical inconsistencies in our beliefs. Take the saying "what is the sound of one hand clapping?" In trying to answer that question we are faced with a logical inconsistency: We are being asked to identify a sound that logic tells us doesn't exist. One such logical dilemma is associated with any concentration training program that attempts to teach you to play in the zone or have a peak experience. To play in the zone, you must respond automatically or unconsciously. Instead of thinking about all of the things that you have to do, you are simply allowing them to happen. By definition, a training program requires your conscious attention—you are trying to make things happen. How, then, do you train yourself to respond automatically?

Actually, the dilemma is not that difficult to resolve. You must do two things. First, remember that thinking automatically isn't an all-or-none process! You are learning to think less and less and to remove more and more task-irrelevant distractions from your thinking. If the training program is working, you are replacing many task-irrelevant thoughts with a few task-relevant ones.

Second, learn to think about concentration skills in the same way that you think about physical skills. If you want to develop a particular physical skill (e.g., throwing), you do that by breaking down the movement sequence. In the throwing example, you identify exercises that will strengthen the different parts of the body that are required for throwing and bring the separate motor segments together into one smooth response. As you practice, your performance becomes more and more automatic. That is what you have to do with the concentration and arousal control exercises that follow. You will be breaking concentration down into separate elements, practicing and developing the parts, and then putting them together. Ultimately, you will be able to perform the entire sequence automatically.

I have tried to define terms carefully in these first six chapters so that you and I can speak the same language. If you have difficulty with any of the terms discussed, refer back to the chapter or look at the glossary at the end of this book.

Summary

Once you have identified a part of your performance or a problem that you want to work on, you need to put that problem in perspective. Too often when difficulties occur, athletes exaggerate them and begin to panic. When this occurs, self-confidence deteriorates in all areas, not just in the specific performance situation. Just taking the time to get a realistic look at your problem will often reduce a great deal of anxiety and result in some immediate performance improvement and an increase in self-confidence.

As you begin to work on a mental skills program, remember that you are engaging in a conscious, mechanical process (just as you do when you develop a new physical skill). Because the process is a conscious one, it will not immediately lead to dramatic performance improvement. That can only occur after you have practiced enough so that mental control (e.g., control over the focus of concentration) becomes as automatic as physical control.

CHAPTER 7

LEARNING TO CONTROL
THE MIND-BODY LINK

Positive images will gradually begin to have greater and greater power to effect the physical and psychological changes you want.

A few years back there was a popular game that children used as a lie detector or to tell the future. The game consisted of a board with a circle on it. Placed around the edge of the circle were words like "yes," "no," and "sometimes," and numbers. The only other piece of equipment was a pendulum, which consisted of a small weight (e.g., a button or fishing weight) attached to the end of a piece of string.

One person would hold the string between his or her thumb and forefinger so that the weight was suspended about half an inch above the center of the circle. The person holding the weight would rest his or her elbow on the table (just off the board) and slightly bend the wrist on the hand holding the pendulum.

A second person would ask a question, and then everyone would wait for the pendulum to begin swinging toward the answer. The individual holding the pendulum would often be convinced that he or she wasn't controlling the movement. Often, children insisted that some spirit was responsible for the movement.

Well, we know that spirits are not responsible for the movement of the pendulum. We also know that the individual holding the pendulum does not have to consciously try to make the pendulum move. What causes the movement? It is really quite simple: The movement is associated with the thoughts of the person holding the pendulum. There are unconscious movements associated with thoughts.

It is fairly easy to demonstrate the relationship between thought and muscle movement using biofeedback. We now have extremely sensitive equipment that can measure the very small electrical changes that occur when muscle neurons fire. Those changes may be only 1/1,000,000th of a volt. By attaching electrodes to muscles in your forehead, shoulders, legs, and so forth, we can measure unconscious changes that occur in response to our saying a word or asking you to think about a particular topic. If we say the word relax, the tension in your muscles will automatically drop.

The neuron firing and muscle movements that are responses to your thoughts are referred to as *ideomotor responses*. The pendulum that was used as a children's game can be thought of as an early version of biofeedback. The suspended weight is quite sensitive to even subtle movements. You can demonstrate this phenomenon to yourself quite easily. All you have to do is construct a pendulum and hold it over a flat surface in the manner indicated at the beginning of this chapter. Then, think about a direction you would like the pendulum to move in (e.g., right to left, up and down, in a circle). Try to will the pendulum to move, that is, think about the movement that you want to make, but don't consciously try to move the pendulum. Simply let the pendulum move.

Ideomotor Responses in Sport

The idea that thought and movement are so closely related shouldn't come as a surprise to an athlete! Athletes work very hard to systematically train their bodies so that they respond with very complete, complex motor sequences to simple thoughts. Consider a gymnast who makes a tumbling run during a floor exercise. The entire sequence, which may include four or five different somersaults and twists, is probably initiated by a single thought.

A boxer throws a combination of punches without consciously thinking about what he is doing. He doesn't think, Left jab, left jab, right to the body, left to the head. His body automatically responds to information that his eyes perceive; he doesn't even have to think of a word.

Ideomotor responses can be either positive or destructive, interfering with the ability to perform. A tennis player who momentarily thinks that her opponent may serve, or hit a shot to a particular side of her body, automatically starts to lean in that direction. If her opponent sees the lean, she hits to the opposite side, winning the point easily, because the other player's thoughts resulted in her being caught off-balance.

Thoughts about trying harder often result in increases in muscle tension that interfere with performance. This muscle tension occurs in not only the muscles that facilitate performance, but also the muscles that oppose those you need to use. You end up working against yourself. This is what happens when a pitcher overthrows and a golfer "muscles" her shot.

Consider the confusion that occurs when your body gets competing messages. I remember playing a game on the diving board at the local swimming pool. I would bounce on the end of the board and then, as I left the board, a person on the side would shout either "Jump," or "Dive." More often than not, I would be anticipating one thing, and he or she would shout the other. As a result of these competing messages, I would try to do both, accomplishing neither. I ended up being trapped between the two, landing on my stomach.

These competing responses occur all the time. The tennis player can't decide which shot to play; the quarterback changes his mind about which of two receivers to throw to. Because each thought entails a highly trained, automatic response, your body behaves in the same confused way that your mind does.

You React to Thoughts You Aren't Even Aware Of!

In the examples presented so far, your thoughts were meant to generate a movement. That is, you thought about what you wanted to have happen. Problems occurred because you guessed wrong, or because you thought about two things at the same time. There are other times, however, when the thought was not intended to create a movement, yet it did.

Through your competitive experiences, you have conditioned your body to react to a lot of thoughts without even realizing it. The thought "Don't hit it into the net" isn't meant to cause you to hit the ball into the net, but the negative images associated with your thoughts create that result. Your negative thoughts result in increased muscle tension and in the unconscious selection of an inappropriate motor sequence. The same thing occurs when you say "Don't miss."

If you anticipate being overpowered or pushed back by an opponent (e.g., an opposing lineman in football), or by an opponent's shot (e.g., in tennis), you automatically start backing up. You become defensive before the first shot is fired. Thinking "she's too good" may result in a whole sequence of motor responses. These responses can make you feel awkward, uncoordinated, slow, heavy, and tired.

Just as negative thoughts result in negative consequences, so, too, can positive thoughts result in positive consequences. Muhammed Ali used to keep himself dancing and jabbing in the ring even when he was tired by saying "Float like a butterfly, sting like a bee." To Ali, the images of floating and stinging were associated with specific automatic movements.

What Gives Images Their Power?

You have the capacity to make images very real. You do this by becoming immersed in them. Simply saying "Float like a butterfly, sting like a bee" isn't enough for most of us. Especially as we are learning, we need to really become immersed in our images, generating all the feelings associated with them. Once we have paired those images with movements and feelings through training, we then begin to shorten the process because we have conditioned a series of responses. Similarly, we shorten the physical or technical instructions we have to give ourselves as we become more physically skilled.

For many athletes, images associated with choking have become more real than images associated with playing well. They have much greater faith in their ability to choke than in their ability to play well. This means that when they have thoughts and feelings associated with choking, it is easy for them to become immersed in the choking thoughts. In contrast, when athletes have thoughts and feelings associated with playing well, it is much easier for them to become immersed in task-relevant cues and to begin playing in the zone.

I remember a basketball player who had lost so much confidence in his ability that he was having a recurring nightmare. He would dream that he was sitting at a table with a basket set up in the middle of the table. He had a basketball in his hand, which he attempted to drop through the basket. Every time he placed his hand over the basket, it would move. In the dream he could feel himself beginning to panic as he tried harder and harder and got nowhere.

The athlete had performed poorly at the start of the season and had lost his starting position as a guard. He was getting very little playing time, and when he did get in the game he felt tremendous pressure to produce immediately. As I explored with him what was going on mentally, he told me that he would start thinking "If I don't get the ball and score quickly, the coach is going to pull me." In response to those thoughts he would feel himself tightening up. The increased tension interfered with his play: He made simple passing mistakes; and he tried to make baskets on fast breaks and missed easy layups, hitting the front of the rim. As a result, he started to freeze and wasn't taking shots when he had the opportunity.

Getting this player to develop positive images was extremely difficult. He associated so many different things with failure that, no sooner would we start to change his reaction to one thought or cue that was creating pressure (e.g., seeing how much time there was on the clock), than he would come up with another (e.g., seeing the coach on the sidelines).

It took several weeks of hard work on his part to reach the point where he was capable of blocking out his negative thoughts and making a serious attempt to score off a fast break. Although he had the personal satisfaction of overcoming some of his anxiety, it was too little, too late as far as the coach was concerned.

The athlete still didn't get to play and ended up quitting the team.

Giving Images Positive Power Over Your Body Requires Work

As the example of the basketball player shows, developing positive images takes a lot of work. One of the reasons for this is that some athletes have spent their careers developing faith in their lack of confidence. They have learned to become immersed in negative thoughts and feelings. All it takes is a couple of key words, or some outcome-related cue (e.g., the amount of time left in the game, or the score), and because they have so much faith in their lack of ability, they are quickly swallowed up (immersed). In contrast, when these athletes try to respond with confidence, they have very little faith. Their lack of faith results in negative thinking and doubts, which keep them from becoming immersed in positive images and attending to the actual situation.

In general, the lower your confidence, the more situations you will have to work on and the harder you will have to work to learn to set aside negative thoughts and feelings and become immersed in positive images. It is possible, however, *provided you stick to one situation at a time*. If you do that, those images will gradually begin to have greater and greater power to effect the physical and psychological changes you want. The first success will be the most difficult. After that, positive changes will begin to occur more quickly, because you will be building the kind of faith required to let you shut out your self-doubts.

When first starting out, you will find that it is hard enough to become immersed in positive feelings when you are in a very calm, quiet, relaxed setting, as opposed to an intense competitive environment. The more you practice, however, the better you will become at gaining control over positive (performance-facilitating) ideomotor responses, and the faster you will be able to develop those feelings.

Sarah was a gymnast with good all-around skills but no real strength. The level of her performance was the same whether she was performing in a floor exercise, on the uneven parallel bars or the beam, or in the vault. She performed well in big competitions against individuals who were superior to her in terms of both level of difficulty and skill. Sarah had most of her problems in competitions where her all-around skill should have given her an advantage over her competitors.

In big competitions, Sarah was a consistent performer. In dual meets against people she should outperform, she was inconsistent. As far as Sarah was concerned, her inconsistency was unpredictable. In one performance she would fall off in the vault, in another it would be the beam.

As Sarah and I discussed her competitions, it became apparent that there was a pattern to her inconsistency. Sarah's performance would drop in those events where she felt one of her competitors was stronger. Somehow, she would lose sight of the fact that the overall outcome of the competition depended upon scores in several events. She was not able to attend to the fact that her all-around skill gave her a big advantage over the competition. Instead, she would feel pressured to match the skill level of the individual who was technically superior in one event.

Sarah would start thinking, "I must perform my best," "I can't make the mistake I made in practice," and "She is really good at X, I will have to be on." Her thoughts would cause her to tighten up and to press. She would lose some height and speed of rotation, and if she really got pumped up, she would overrotate. Her body was automatically reacting to her negative thoughts.

In big competitions against people who should beat her, Sarah didn't have the same problem. She wasn't expected to win, so she didn't put the same kind of pressure on herself. As a result, she would often perform above the level expected, at least until she would become aware that she had a chance to win. Then something would happen that caused her to lose.

Sarah's behavior is not unlike that of tennis players who can't seem to win the big point or who have particular parts of their game fall apart (e.g., the backhand) when they play against opponents they view as having a bigger weapon (in that particular area). It's the same process that keeps the basketball player from making critical free throws, and results in a pitcher's walking batters when the team is only an out or two away from a victory.

Sarah was able to gain control over her negative thinking and to win those competitions that she was expected to win. To do it, however, she had to work on controlling her thoughts in relationship to particular athletes and particular competitions. For example, she would spend a week working on positive thinking on the balance beam, when one of her competitors that week was particularly strong in this area. Sarah's focus was not on beating the opposition, but on controlling concentration and performing up to her own potential, independent of her competitors' performances.

Summary

Ideomotor responses are muscular changes or reactions that occur in response to images or thoughts. For example, the thought "don't lose" often results in physiological changes that cause the athlete to assume a defensive position, rather than an offensive one. Chapter 9 teaches you how to control ideomotor responses through self-hypnosis and how to transfer that control from the hypnotic state to the actual performance situation. Before you begin the self-hypnosis exercises, however, you need to understand the importance of centering, discussed in chapter 8. This is because unconscious ideomotor responses affect your ability to perform by altering your center of gravity. You will learn to use both self-hypnosis and key or trigger words to help you center yourself. This process clears your mind, controls physiological tension, and helps you enter the zone.

CHAPTER 8

CENTERING TO CONTROL COORDINATION AND TIMING

His center of mass was involuntarily shifted too far back on his skis. His weight was off his skis, but he made an unbelievable recovery.

The concept of *centering* comes from the martial arts and refers to a process used to create feelings of being grounded, calm, relaxed, receptive (e.g., to stimuli), and clear (in thought). Being centered is the opposite of being anxious or upset. When you are anxious, you lack confidence, can't think clearly, are confused and worried and so forth. Your *center of mass*, or *one point*, is a spot located just below (1 or 2 inches) and behind your navel. That point has great significance in sport and physical activity. That is the point you momentarily and *consciously* attend to in order to center yourself.

Importance of the One Point or Center of Mass

When you are centered, your knees are slightly bent, your muscles are loose (slightly relaxed, but ready), and your breathing is steady and slightly deeper and slower than normal. In addition, your weight is evenly distributed between your two feet, which are approximately 18 inches apart, one slightly in front of the other. This position results in a sense of being balanced—of being ready to move in any direction. Any alteration in your center of mass results in a loss of that feeling of balance and of your ability to move equally well in any direction.

Remaining balanced, keeping a relatively low center of mass, and getting that center of mass to move through the activity you are engaging in all give power to movement. Perhaps a few examples will help you understand what I mean.

Consider a boxer who wants to deliver a punch. If the boxer raises his center of mass by straightening up (locking his knees) before throwing a punch, he cannot get his weight behind the punch. To feel this, stand on your tiptoes with your knees locked, and jab as if you were trying to hit someone. You should notice that under these conditions there is very little power in your jab. All of the power is being generated by your arm, and none of your weight gets behind the punch. In contrast, if you begin with a lower center of mass (knees bent) and transfer your weight by raising your center of mass as you jab, then you have the full weight of your body behind the punch. The same is true for hitting a baseball, golf ball, or tennis ball (see Figure 8.1). This transfer of weight, the shifting of your center of mass, gives you power.

When a tennis player or a hitter becomes defensive, his thoughts cause him to move his center of mass backward. This means more of his weight is centered over his back foot. If he can quickly move his feet back into position (get his feet under him) and then transfer his weight forward at the right time, he will generate a great deal of power. When he thinks defensively, however, he not only gets the weight onto his back foot, but also tends to straighten up. This causes him to be off-balance and fall backward. From this position, he has no power when he tries to hit the ball. His body is moving away from the ball, and he is trying to do everything with his arm. For an example of the right way to do this, watch how Steffi Graf and Michael Chang maintain their balance and manage to shift their weight forward just as they make contact with the ball.

In most sports, it is critical that you maintain your balance, keeping your feet under you and rotating around your center of

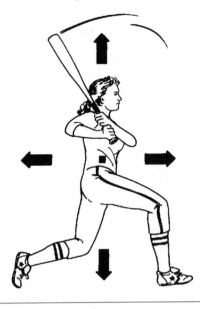

Figure 8.1
Movement around your center of mass.

mass (e.g., gymnastics, diving, discus, and shotput). The athlete who feels pressured and rushed has a tendency to shift her weight forward just a little early. She doesn't bend her knees, and she brings her center of mass up too high. In addition, she leans forward, getting too much weight out in front. As a consequence, she is off-balance, falling forward. When this happens in tennis, the player hits the ball in the net. The boxer doesn't recover from his jab (by getting his feet under himself quickly enough) and lunges forward. At this point, he is off-balance and extremely vulnerable to a counterpunch.

The overaggressive defensive lineman in football comes up too high and leans too much. He is off-balance and an easy mark for the smart offensive lineman, who simply uses a little leverage to cause the defensive player to lose his balance and fall on his face. When they don't remain centered, the diver, the gymnast, and the high jumper don't get the knee bend they need to obtain maximum power from their take off. This is what happens in these sports when you start feeling the pressure. Your center of mass raises up too high, too early!

What Affects Your Center of Mass?

When you find yourself feeling off-balance and uncoordinated, it is because thoughts have altered your center of mass. When you are in the zone, the thoughts that you are having are either helping you maintain your balance, or they are neutral (not affecting your center of mass). Some examples will help you understand the differences in the feelings that you have when your center of mass is disturbed by thoughts, as opposed to when it is disturbed by actual physical changes you have to react to.

In the 1988 Winter Olympics, I watched a skier competing in the giant slalom. As the individual came down the hill, it was easy to see that he was balanced (over his skis). He was moving extremely well through the gates and in control of everything that was going on. Suddenly, he hit a very icy patch, and his skis slid to the side and out in front. His center of mass was involuntarily shifted too far back on his skis. His weight was off his skis, behind his center of mass. In this particular instance, the skier made an unbelievable recovery. Somehow, he managed to pull his skis back underneath him and recenter himself. He finished the run and won a medal. This individual was in control throughout the race. He was centered until something threw him off balance. At that point, he recovered automatically (because of experience and great skill), recentered, and finished the race.

When you are choking, and when you are being knocked off-balance by your own thoughts, you have shaky, unstable feelings even when standing still. Your breathing is rapid and shallow, and muscle tension has increased throughout your body. The normal knee-bend you have when you are comfortable and centered is reduced. As you perform, things get even worse.

For example, a tennis player who is in the zone sees the whole court. She is immersed in external cues, which not only enables her to see the court, but helps her feel as if things are happening more slowly. Because she sees the whole court, she is better able to anticipate her opponent's moves. She doesn't move any faster from Point A to Point B than normal, but she starts sooner because of her improved ability to anticipate. The early start allows her to get in position early; she is always balanced and always able to set up, keeping her feet under her. As she hits the ball, she transfers her weight at just the right moment, using all of the power in her body.

On a normal day, she has more distractions and isn't seeing the court quite as well. She anticipates well and sets up early for some shots, but is a little slow starting for others. As a result, she finds herself stretching and reaching for more balls. She is off-balance on more shots, not able to get her weight into the ball. Her performance is inconsistent.

When this player is very anxious, she has even more distractions. She picks up the ball later, and she has a harder time moving because of increased muscle tension. She never feels completely balanced. When she isn't watching the ball, she picks it up late and finds herself falling backward, in an attempt to find more time to hit the ball. With her weight moving in the opposite direction of her swing, she has no power in her shot. In fact, she will be lucky if the ball gets to the net. The late starts and the feeling of being pushed backward cause her to panic and to feel rushed. Now, when she does see the ball early enough to move, she moves too quickly. She plants her feet too soon, starting her swing too early, and ends up leaning forward, shifting weight too far forward, and falling off-balance (like the boxer who lunges); once again she fails to get her weight into the ball. Her weight has already moved as far forward as it can go before her racquet makes contact with the ball. This athlete has rushed her preparation and her shot.

Learning to Center Is the Key to Performing Well

Just as thoughts can negatively alter your center of mass, so, too, can they help you reestablish that feeling of being centered. One of your challenges is to identify a couple of trigger (key) words that you associated with being centered. You will use these words to trigger that feeling in actual performance situations.

Table 8.1 lists some of the words that other athletes have found useful in describing the mental and physical feelings they have when choking and when playing their best. Look at those words and see which ones best describe your feelings under each of the conditions.

Table 8.1 divides words into two groups: those that reflect physiological feelings (e.g., tense), and those that reflect perceptual

Table 8.1   Feelings Associated With Altered States

Physical feelings		Psychological feelings	
The zone	Choking	The zone	Choking
Loose	Tight	Controlled	Beaten
Relaxed	Tense	Confident	Scared
Solid	Shaky	Powerful	Weak
Balanced	Unsteady	Commanding	Dominated
Strong	Weak	Calm	Upset
Light	Heavy	Tranquil	Panicked
Energetic	Tired	Peaceful	Worried
Effortless	Hard	Easy	Rushed
Fluid	Choppy	Clear	Confused
Smooth	Awkward	Focused	Overloaded

processes (e.g., focused, clear) or a state of mind (e.g., calm). In addition, each word listed in "The zone" category has its opposite in the "Choking" category (e.g., relaxed vs. tense, confident vs. scared).

Your task is to pick one word from each of the zone categories. Pick the words that best describe your own feelings (e.g., fluid and confident, or strong and controlling). If you don't find a word that you like, then come up with your own. What the word communicates to other people isn't important. What the word communicates to you is critical. You want to find the two words that are most powerfully associated with playing at your best. Which two words seem to have the strongest emotional impact on you? You are going to be using those words in the exercises that follow. It is important to limit yourself to just two words. Those two words, through training, will eventually act as triggers to help you quickly establish a feeling of being centered when you find yourself off-balance.

Let me describe how these cue words work by giving you an example involving a multievent athlete in track-and-field. This particular individual felt that his greatest strength was his explosive power. Thus he scored well in sprints and in the throws. When it came to the 1,500-meter run, however, he lacked confidence. He would attempt to compensate for his negative feelings by trying to overpower the event. Instead of running relaxed, he would tighten up. Individuals running with him could see him straighten up, running with a shorter, choppy stride.

Looking over the list of trigger words, the athlete settled on *fluid* and *easy* to alter his running style and to relax in the 1,500. He identified different stages in the race (e.g., the start, the end of the first 100 meters, and the completion of each lap) where he wanted to use self-hypnosis to program himself to center and use his trigger words to elicit the desired responses. He was successful in doing this and improved his personal record in the event by some 10 seconds.

A second example involved a competitor in the sport of wrestling. This individual had a tendency to lose intensity as the match progressed, especially if he had a lead. He had lost several matches in the last few seconds by protecting a lead instead of continuing to be aggressive. To help him maintain his intensity, he chose the words *strong* and *controlling*. He then used self-hypnosis and centering to get him to use these cue words every time there was a break in the action (e.g., when the referee would stop the action, or when there would be a momentary lull in the action as each wrestler caught his breath).

Summary

When you are in control and feeling confident in a performance situation you are *centered*. Being centered is dependent upon your center of mass, or one point, being ideally positioned for the particular performance setting you are in. In some settings, your center of mass will be lower than in others (e.g., when you don't want to be moved easily). In some settings, your center of mass will be farther forward than in others (e.g., when you want to take the offensive or get a quick start).

Thought processes often interfere with an athlete's ability to feel centered or ready. Centering is the breathing and attentional refocusing process that you go through when preparing to perform in order to become centered. It is this process that sets the stage for optimal performance.

At first, the process of centering will be conscious and mechanical. And, once you are centered, it won't be long before new thoughts or feelings cause ideomotor responses that throw you off-balance. However, with practice and the use of trigger words, the process will become quicker and more automatic, and you will be able to maintain freedom from distractions for longer periods of time.

CHAPTER 9

SELF-HYPNOSIS: DEVELOPING PERSONALIZED TRAINING SCRIPTS

Just as the pitcher would go into his windup, the batter would silently say "Balanced and focused."

What is self-hypnosis, and how does it differ from relaxation procedures and mental rehearsal? There isn't a simple answer to that question. A number of researchers insist that there aren't any differences and that anything that can be done through the use of self-hypnosis can be done without it. Others insist that a qualitative difference exists between the two states. I believe that the difference exists in the mind of the subject; no real difference exists between the procedures. This doesn't mean that the distinction isn't real to the subject. It's as genuine as the distinction between feeling confident and feeling frightened.

Imagine becoming so sick that you get frightened. You feel weak, faint, and tired. You have been doing a lot of reading and are sure that you have some terminal illness. Finally, you become so scared that you begin to tell people about your symptoms and your concerns. You describe your symptoms to a relative, who listens carefully and then tells you that he had the same thing last month, so you shouldn't worry. Does that advice reduce your anxiety and help you regain control? That depends on the level of confidence you place in your relative's opinion.

Consider the same situation, only this time you go to a doctor with an excellent reputation. Like your relative, the doctor listens to the symptoms and then says you have a viral infection that has been going around. She informs you that there really isn't any treatment other than rest, and that the symptoms will pass in a week or two.

Your anxiety probably will be somewhat reduced in both situations. If you are like most of us, however, your anxiety will be reduced more by the doctor than it will by your relative. You are much more likely to have faith in the doctor because of her training and reputation. The same thing applies when we compare self-hypnosis with relaxation and mental rehearsal.

Why Self-Hypnosis?

I have chosen to teach you self-hypnosis because many people have a stronger belief in the technique's ability to help them than they do in relaxation and mental rehearsal. If that is true for you, then your belief will make it easier (at the start) for you to cooperate, to respond to suggestions, and to become immersed.

I don't know why many athletes have greater initial confidence in self-hypnosis procedures than they do in various forms of relaxation. I do know what they see as different between the two. First, they describe the hypnotic experience as deeper or more real. They feel as if they were "really there" during the hypnosis. In effect, they are more immersed in their imagery. It's possible that hypnosis allows them to let go and gives them more freedom to fantasize. It's also possible that the word *hypnosis* carries with it an aura that captures their interest and helps them focus on their images.

In any case, many athletes encounter fewer distractions with self-hypnosis, and thus immersion is more complete. A runner described it this way:

When I was using relaxation procedures I wasn't really convinced they would work. I kept questioning why I was doing the things I was doing, and I kept arguing with myself. With hypnosis it was different. I had a couple of friends who had been to a hypnotist and turned in some really good times. I had heard some good things from my coach about athletes it had helped. I was eager to try it and just found it easy to let go.

Any advantage that self-hypnosis might have over relaxation, mental rehearsal, and meditation is short-lived unless you faithfully follow the exercise. Your initial belief in the procedure can be a big help, but if you don't work to build faith by committing yourself to practice even in the face of doubt, then, in the long run, nothing will change. Similarly, if you stick religiously to a relaxation or mental rehearsal procedure, you can derive the same benefits, provided the content of the different procedures is essentially the same.

In addition to a confidence, or belief factor, I have chosen to teach you self-hypnosis for three other reasons. First, with self-hypnosis you grow to accept control and responsibility. You are allowed some dependency at the start (e.g., on taped procedures), and you are provided with structure. At the same time, you are encouraged to take more and more responsibility. For this reason, the problems about trust and dependency that can develop in relationships with other people (e.g., a hypnotist) are less likely to occur.

Second, self-hypnosis emphasizes that becoming immersed is a skill you can develop. A goal of training is to learn to become so immersed in images and sensations, that you feel as if they were real. As you develop this skill, you begin to feel as if you were actually having the necessary successes to increase your self-confidence and faith in your ability to play in the zone and to win.

Third, self-hypnosis is easily structured so that you can give yourself posthypnotic suggestions that will facilitate the transfer of your feelings and experiences in the hypnotic state to the actual performance situation.

Training Goals

The goal of training is to help you develop the necessary skills for controlling concentration and arousal so that you can perform unconsciously or automatically. Training helps you quiet the inner voices that keep you from becoming immersed and concentrating effectively. Training helps you stay centered and gives you more control over the ideomotor changes that interfere with your coordination, timing, and power.

Put the Training Procedures on Tape

Later in the chapter is a script for you to put onto a tape that you can listen to. The tape helps you enter a hypnotic state and teaches you to become immersed in your competitive environment. Listening to the tape is only a first step. The intent is for you to develop your concentration skills and to learn the procedure well enough to induce a hypnotic state without listening to the tape.

The tape is helpful at first because it provides you with some structure and keeps you from worrying about what happens next. The fewer worries and doubts you have, the easier it is for you to become immersed in, and responsive to, the suggestions on the tape.

As your skills develop, several things will occur:

- Your images and associated sensations will become more vivid.
- You will no longer need the tape to enter a hypnotic state.
- The speed with which you achieve a state of immersion will increase to the point where you will be able to accomplish it within the time required to take one or two deep breaths.
- You will be able to become immersed under increasingly stressful conditions.

When you put the procedures on a tape, read them in a firm, steady voice. Don't be overly dramatic, but read them slowly, pacing them so that you have time to respond (imagine you are responding while you are reading). The tape should be somewhere between 10 and 20 minutes in length when you finish.

Occasionally, an athlete is uncomfortable listening to his or her own voice. If this is true for you, you might want to have someone else read the procedures onto a tape for you.

Exercise Components

The procedure is actually composed of five phases, each of which has been included for a reason. Once you begin to develop these skills and take yourself through them in the absence of a tape, you will want to increase or decrease the amount of time you spend on any given part of the exercise. The five components of the exercise are as follows:

1. Developing and becoming immersed in an ideomotor response
2. Developing a state of muscular relaxation
3. Centering and shifting attention from *soft eyes* to *hard eyes*
4. Immersing yourself and playing in the zone
5. Giving suggestions to transfer your feelings and control over concentration to an actual performance situation

It's not uncommon for an athlete to say "Everything is okay, except my legs feel tired." If your legs feel tired (lethargic, lacking the spring you want), everything isn't okay. Few sports don't rely heavily upon your legs. Speed, coordination, timing, and power all depend upon what goes on in your lower body. An athlete whose legs feel tired and lethargic is going to struggle to concentrate. Negative thoughts are much more likely to occur and will be much harder to get rid of.

Phase 1 of the training program teaches you to induce feelings of both heaviness and lightness in your body. Learning to do this gives you a real advantage in sport settings. You have probably been in performance situations where you felt tired and lethargic and needed a physical lift. Other times when you felt anxious you needed to feel heavier or more grounded. This phase teaches you to use immersion to create whichever feeling you need to recenter yourself.

The second phase provides you with a strategy for relaxing when you are away from an actual competition and helping you concentrate during this first part of your training program. You can reduce or eliminate this phase as you become more skilled at quickly relaxing and focusing your concentration.

Phase 3 is sport specific. I have prepared several different scripts for this portion of your training (see chapter 10). If your particular sport is not represented, then use one of the scripts provided here as a model to guide you in the development of your own sport-specific script.

The third phase emphasizes making you consciously aware of the shifting of attention that needs to occur in your sport when you are playing in the zone. Because you are in the zone, you will not need to shift from an external focus to an internal one. The width of your attentional focus will change automatically, however, from a broad focus to a narrow focus in response to changing performance demands. Although you won't want to have to consciously think about this when you are actually performing (it should occur automatically), you need to learn how to make adjustments and corrections when things aren't going well.

Most athletes learn to concentrate by trial and error. They may engage in the correct process, while not knowing what that process is. When something interferes with their performances (e.g., when they start to feel the pressure and choke), they don't know how to regain control. Phase 3 teaches you what to do—more specifically, what to attend to—when things aren't going your way. Remember, this method applies only when you are having problems controlling concentration and tension, not when your problem is a simple technical issue.

Phase 4 involves mentally rehearsing what happens when you play in the zone. The goal is to become progressively more immersed in the imagery (thoughts, feelings, and sensations) and to learn to make this experience more and more real. As your imagery becomes more vivid, it begins to affect your confidence and performance in the actual situation. As the experience becomes more vivid, faith in your ability to play in the zone will grow.

In the fifth phase, you use centering and the key words you chose in chapter 8 to help you maintain your center of mass. You will then use these words in actual performance situations to control concentration and arousal.

Practicing and Using Training Procedures

To learn these procedures, listen to the tape twice a day for a week. During the second week, listen to the tape once each day, and then take yourself through the procedures a second time without the tape. Once you have developed the skills to become immersed on your own, I would still recommend that you rehearse twice a day. You can shorten the length of time for mentally rehearsing (e.g., by cutting out the relaxation phase), but don't cut it to less than 10 minutes. Add any time you save by shortening Phases 1, 2, and 3 to Phases 4 and 5. Remember, this commitment is necessary to develop genuine confidence and faith!

Sometimes you might have difficulty concentrating on the procedures. As you become more familiar with them, they can become boring. To avoid boredom and maintain concentration, change the script whenever necessary. You may also find that you fall asleep if you lie down while going through the procedures. If this occurs, practice while sitting up. Remember, you are using these procedures not to relax or to fall asleep, but to learn to improve concentration, quiet doubts and distractions, and control physiological arousal.

Here is an example of how to modify the procedures. A hitter in baseball wanted to improve his concentration at the plate. He had a tendency to become physically tight when he had to hit with men on base. At those times, he also tended to think too much and overanalyze the situation. His coach described his problem as one of paralysis by analysis. This athlete would end up either swinging late or being called out on strikes far too often.

He picked the trigger words *balanced* and *focused* to use when he was at bat. We developed a self-hypnosis tape that he used to center himself just after stepping into the batter's box. Then, just as the pitcher would go into his windup, the athlete would silently say "Balanced and focused." This triggered him to release muscle tension and focus his attention on the release point (the spot where the pitcher lets go of the ball).

This individual's concentration improved very quickly, and he started making much better contact with the ball. He was enthusiastic about the program and practiced it religiously. Then, for some reason, he found his old problem returning.

After talking to him and watching him in a game, I realized that his procedure had become so automatic that it had lost its effectiveness in pressure situations. He was centering and saying the words, but they had lost their meaning for him. I suggested

that he find two new words to substitute into his regular procedure. He chose *loose* and *seams*. He explained that seams would
remind him to sharpen his focus and see the ball more clearly.
With this modification, his hitting improved once again.

Practice in the Performance Situation

In addition to practicing the procedures away from the competitive environment, work on using parts of them in the actual
competitive situation, specifically, Phases 3 and 5.

Phase 3 involves identifying when you need to shift from a
broad-external to a narrow-external focus of attention, and then
practicing that shifting. Set aside a part of your actual practice
session (e.g., a 10-minute period on the basketball floor, golf
course, or tennis court) to work on nothing but controlling the
shifting of attention. Your primary goal during this period is to
be able to say that you did make the appropriate shifts—nothing
else matters. Stop working on technique, stop worrying about
the outcome, and concentrate only on controlling attentional
shifts.

In baseball, the hitter centers when he first gets into the
batter's box. He broadens attention (soft eyes) and assesses the
situation, becoming aware of the positions of the infield, the
outfield, and any base runners. He looks to the coach for signals.
Then, as the pitcher goes into his windup, he uses his key words
to control tension and effect an attentional shift. Concentration
narrows and becomes focused on the release point.

Practice Phase 5 in a similar way. Designate a few minutes
during practice when you are going to consciously forget about
technique and outcome and concentrate only on centering. Work
on using breathing and your key phrases to get yourself immersed in the process of playing. This quiets your internal voice!

A tennis player is working on her backhand and begins to get
frustrated at what seems to be a lack of progress. She realizes
that her frustration is increasing tension. This provides her with
an opportunity to use the centering technique to try to control
arousal and any related mental distractions. Although she continues working on the backhand, she alters her goals. The outcome
of the backhand practice becomes secondary to reducing tension
and getting rid of negative thoughts. She gains control over her

attitude, and this is reflected in the way she walks, talks, and looks on the court.

At first, you may need to limit your work on these two phases to times during practice when you are feeling confident and good about things. As you begin to develop your skills, however, it's important to practice these phases when you are having problems as well. That way, you can discipline yourself to use the procedures in situations similar to those that you run into during competitions when you are frustrated and upset. It won't be easy, but faithful practice will pay off, just as it does for physical skills. If you are working with a coach or teammates, involve them in your mental training. You need to be able to practice focusing concentration and making attentional shifts independent of the outcome. That will be impossible, unless your coach or teammates agree with and support your goal.

Applications Within the Performance Situation

When you are playing well, you won't need to consciously attend to the procedures that you are learning. Your performance will be mostly automatic, and any adjustments you make will happen very quickly.

When you are not playing well, you will be making use of Phases 3 and 5. In tennis, for example, you can use the time both between points and on changeovers between games to remind yourself of the attentional shifts you should be making and to use your key words to center when you begin to lose control over concentration and arousal.

You won't have the time during a game to go through the entire 10- to 20-minute procedure. But if the level of relaxation you achieve during the full procedure is fairly deep, you probably wouldn't want to go through the entire procedure anyway. You might become too relaxed.

Preparing Yourself for Hypnosis

When you listen to the tape, find a place where you won't be disturbed. This is because distractions make it difficult for you to learn. You need to know that no matter how deeply hypnotized you become, you will be in control of everything, remember everything, and be able to respond appropriately to any situation or interference that might arise. Find a place to sit or lie down where you won't have to worry about responding to the telephone, the doorbell, or any other interruption. This enables you to concentrate better.

Do everything you can to make it easier to concentrate on, and respond to, the suggestions on the tape. Remember, becoming hypnotized and immersed is a skill that you develop. If your feelings aren't as intense as you had hoped, don't be concerned. Continued practice will help you develop the level of skill you want.

One additional point. I have told you that being immersed and playing in the zone occur on a continuum. Some distractions are likely to occur when you are practicing, but how you react to those distractions is far more important than the distractions themselves. Let's look at one common distraction that occurs when individuals are being hypnotized for the first time.

The individual who is being hypnotized for the first time is usually excited and cooperative. A common problem is for that person to check up on him- or herself to see if the suggestions are having the desired effect. For example, let's say you have suggested to yourself that your arm is heavy. Ideally, you would passively attend to your arm and allow those feelings to develop by calling up the suggested images. When you are trying this for the first time, however, you might want to check to see if your arm is responding to your suggestion. Doing this distracts you and slows down immersion. The distraction would be okay, if it ended there and you returned your attention to the images. Too often, inexperienced subjects expect too much too soon. When you check to see if your arm has responded, and it hasn't, you might become upset and distracted by thoughts about why the hypnosis isn't working.

Distractions Are Inevitable But Unimportant

When distractions occur, just let them go. If they require a response (e.g., if you need to move to get more comfortable or scratch an itch), it's okay to respond. You will learn that you can respond without affecting your ability to become immersed.

Letting go of these distractions is excellent concentration practice for what you need to do in performance situations. Golfers will hit bad shots, and tennis players will double-fault. Superior athletes learn to let these inevitable mistakes (potential distractions) go, so that they don't affect subsequent performance. Remember, you learn from mistakes and distractions, not from error-free performances. Errors provide you with an opportunity to practice gaining control over unwanted distractions and disruptive ideomotor responses!

Now it's time to pick a quiet spot, to turn on your tape recorder, and to read the following script.

Self-Hypnosis Script[1]

PHASE 1

Close your eyes, and begin by taking three deep breaths. Inhale deeply, and exhale slowly. . . . Inhale deeply, and exhale slowly. . . . Inhale deeply and exhale slowly. That's fine, . . . now just relax, let yourself go, and know that no matter how deeply hypnotized you become, you will always be in control and able to respond to anything that you choose to respond to. . . . No matter how deeply hypnotized you become, you will remember everything.

Begin to concentrate on your right arm.[2] . . . Position your right arm so that your hand is open, and your palm is facing up. . . . That's fine. . . . Now pay attention to the feelings in your upper arm, . . . in your forearm, . . . in your hand and fingers. Notice any sensations that may be occurring in your right arm. . . . You may feel a breeze blowing across the hairs. You may feel a tingling sensation in your hand or fingers. Just observe the feelings. . . .

Now, notice the feelings of heaviness that occur in your right arm as you exhale. . . . Just relax, and notice the feeling

---

[1]My original procedures have been modified since reading an excellent book on self-hypnosis by David A. Soskis, *Teaching Self-Hypnosis: An Introductory Guide for Clinicians.* Prior to reading Dr. Soskis's book, I had not been using the ideomotor demonstrations, nor the hand levitation. The relevance of these two procedures to work with athletes was obvious, and I have found the addition quite helpful.

[2]If you are sitting, extend your arm out in front of you. If you are laying down lift your arm so that you have to support its weight.

*of comfortable, relaxed, heaviness that develops in your right
arm as you exhale. . . .*

*Take your left arm and position it so that your fingers are
open, but your palm is facing down. . . .* [Repeat this sentence
to give yourself time to respond.] *Make a slight bend in your
left wrist. . . . Good. . . . Now, pay attention to the feelings
in your left hand. Notice as you inhale how your hand begins
to feel lighter. . . . Just relax, and notice as you inhale how
your hand begins to feel lighter, as if it wants to lift up. . . .*

*You can create different feelings in your hands if you want
to, all you have to do is find the right images. . . . Do that
now. Pay attention to your right hand again. Find an image
that helps you develop the feeling of heaviness in your right
hand. Imagine that you are closing your right hand around
a weight, and that the weight is pulling your hand down,
making it heavier, . . . and heavier, . . . heavier, . . . and
heavier. . . . Just let yourself go, and find an image that makes
your right arm feel heavier and heavier with each exhalation.*

*That's fine. . . . Get rid of that image and let the feelings
of heaviness go. . . . Now, pay attention to your left arm.
Imagine a friend reaching out and taking hold of your wrist
between thumb and forefinger. Imagine that each time you
inhale, your friend gently tugs on your wrist, making it feel
lighter . . . and lighter. . . . Each time you inhale, your friend
gently tugs on your wrist pulling it higher . . . and higher,
. . . making it lighter. . . . and lighter. . . . Good. Notice how
much lighter your wrist has become. Find another image that
will make your wrist and arm feel even lighter. . . . Take some
time and develop the feelings of lightness in your left hand. . .*

ALLOW A 2-MINUTE BREAK HERE FOR FEEL-
INGS TO DEVELOP.

PHASE 2

*Good. Now just relax. If your left arm has moved, settle it
back down into a comfortable position. As your arm settles
down, you will feel very comfortable. . . . You can increase*

this pleasant comfortable feeling by counting from one to five. . . . With each count you will become more relaxed and more deeply hypnotized. No matter how deeply hypnotized you become, however, you will always be in control. . . . With each count you will become more relaxed and more deeply hypnotized. No matter how deeply hypnotized you become, however, you will always be in control. . . .

One, . . . relax all of the muscles in both of your arms, in the fingers, . . . hands, . . . forearms, . . . and upper arms. . . . Just completely relax those muscles and enjoy the pleasant feeling of heaviness that occurs as you exhale and sink down deeper and deeper. . . . Two, . . . relax the muscles in both legs. . . . Relax the muscles in your feet and toes. . . . Relax the muscles in your calves. . . . Relax the muscles in your thighs. . . . Just completely relax all of the muscles in both arms and both legs, and notice as you exhale . . . the pleasant sensation of drifting down deeper and deeper, . . . into a deep hypnotic state.

Three, . . . relax all of the muscles in your forehead, . . . cheeks, . . . and jaw. . . . Let your mouth open slightly as you relax the muscles in your jaw. . . . That's fine. . . .

Four, . . . relax the muscles in your neck. . . . Relax the muscles in your shoulders. . . . Just completely relax, drifting down deeper, . . . deeper, . . . still deeper. . . . Five, . . . relax the muscles in your chest, . . . back, . . . and stomach. . . . Relax all of your muscles and enjoy the pleasant sensations of being deeply hypnotized. . . . For the next few moments just let yourself go completely, and with each exhale drift down deeper and deeper. . . . With each exhale. . . drift down deeper. . . and deeper. . . .

ALLOW A 1-MINUTE BREAK HERE.

PHASE 3 (Tennis Specific)

Now, . . . imagine that you are about to serve. . . . As you prepare to serve, look to the other side of the court. . . . You have soft eyes, . . . seeing your opponent waiting to receive serve. At the same time, you can see the entire court. . . . You can see everything. . . . As you stand there, you decide where you will serve, . . . and you make up your mind that you are going to stay back on this point, to play from the baseline. . . .

You can feel the ball in your hand. . . . You can feel its texture and weight. . . . You can feel the seams where there isn't any fuzz. Notice the feeling of your racquet in your hand as you grip it. . . . Notice how tightly you hold it. Notice how it feels against your palms. . . and your fingertips. . . .

Pay attention to your weight distribution. . . . Notice how your center of mass shifts toward your front foot as you bounce the ball and prepare to serve. . . . You feel very comfortable and balanced. . . . Now, as you begin your toss, your attention narrows and you focus on the spot where you are tossing the ball. . . . As your concentration narrows, you see the ball come into view very clearly. You can see the fuzz on the ball, . . . see its color, . . . see it rotate. . . . As you watch the ball, you can feel your racquet coming through, and you see it as it comes into your field of vision. You can see it make contact with the ball, and you can feel your weight and your center of mass transferring, moving forward, coming through at the moment your racquet contacts the ball. . . . Now, you feel the follow-through of your racquet.

Quickly, your attention broadens again and you see the whole court. You can feel yourself recenter as you bring your legs under you. You feel balanced and centered. Your racquet is up and you are ready to move in any direction. . . .

PHASE 4 (Tennis Specific)

That's fine. Now just play some points so things can happen at their regular speed. . . . Let your imagination go. . . . Get completely involved in the points. . . . You will feel and see everything as if you were actually playing the points. . . . You will feel confident, . . . in control. . . . It's easy to move and to get into position, to feel your weight move through the ball with each stroke. . . . You seem to have all the time in the world to prepare. . . . You know that you can do anything you want to with the ball. . . . Just let yourself play, enjoying all of the feelings and sensations that come when you are in the zone. . . .

LEAVE 2 MINUTES HERE FOR MENTAL
REHEARSAL.

PHASE 5 (Tennis Specific)

*That's fine. In a moment it will be time to leave this pleasant
state of hypnosis. . . . Before you do, however, you need to
know that you will be able to create the feelings that you
have when you are playing in the zone whenever you want.
. . . You will be able to do this by taking a deep, centering
breath, . . . inhaling deeply, . . . and attending to the
expansion of the muscles in your abdomen as you inhale. As
you exhale, . . . relax your chest, neck, and shoulder muscles
and say "_____ and _____"* [insert your two trigger words].

*Remember, whenever you want to settle yourself down and
to improve your concentration. . . you simply take a deep,
centering breath. . . . Then, on the exhale say to yourself,
"_____ and _____ ." . . .*

*Imagine yourself going through that process right now. . . .
Imagine you are about to serve in a match. . . . You can feel
the pressure. . . . You are a little tight in your neck and
shoulders. . . . You notice that you are gripping the racquet
a little too tightly, . . . and you are worried about getting
your serve in. . . . Feel the pressure. . . . Now, look at the
court. . . and look across the net. . . .*

*As you look across the net, take that centering breath . . .
and repeat your phrase. . . . At the end of the exhale, notice
that you have soft eyes. . . . You see the whole court. . . . You
feel comfortable. . . . If you like, you may take one more
centering breath, and repeat your phrase just before you
begin your ball toss. . . . Then, . . . as you toss the ball, your
concentration narrows and you focus on the spot where you
are tossing the ball. . . .*

GIVE YOURSELF A MINUTE FOR PRACTICE
HERE.

*Alright, . . . it's time to return to your normal activities.
. . . To do that, count from three to one. . . . On the count of
three, . . . take a deep breath, holding it momentarily. . . .
On the count of two, . . . stretch your arms and legs and
exhale. . . . On the count of one, . . . open your eyes and you
will be wide awake, . . . ready to do the things you normally
do at this time. . . . You're feeling good, . . . comfortable, . . .
and relaxed. . . . Ready. . . . Three, . . . take a deep breath
. . . . Two, . . . stretch your arms and legs and exhale. . . .
One, . . . Open your eyes, wide awake!*

Summary

Self-hypnosis is a technique that allows you to become more totally
immersed in your thoughts and feelings. When self-hypnosis
differs from other rehearsal strategies (e.g., mental rehearsal), it
is because the process of self-hypnosis has led to a greater breakdown in the normal shifting of attention from an external to
internal focus. As you spend progressively more time internally
focused, the images and feelings become more intense and real.

It's important for you to practice self-hypnosis on a regular
basis if you expect to be able to transfer your ability to center
and refocus concentration to actual performance settings. The
use of your key words will assist this process by helping to create
an automatic response.

It's important that you don't limit your mental rehearsal to
those times when you are practicing your self-hypnosis exercises.
There is no reason that you can't rehearse centering and performing a particular response anytime, any place. Really great
athletes are thinking about and mentally practicing their performances almost every waking moment. When there is a lull in
conversation, or when boredom creeps in, they begin to think
about that thing which is most important to them, their performance. The critical thing for you to remember is that your
thoughts at these times should be systematic and focused. You
aren't dreaming, you are performing.

CHAPTER 10

MODIFYING YOUR MENTAL TRAINING PROCEDURES AS YOU PROGRESS

Move smoothly through each of the critical transition points: As the ball comes through, your weight smoothly shifts back toward the center and upward.

Obviously, you will want to make many changes in the wording of the procedure when you begin to induce the hypnotic state yourself (e.g., using "I" instead of "you"). Feel free to alter the images, lengthen or shorten particular phases, and identify other performance sequences that you mentally rehearse. Do not, however, alter the overall structure of the procedures. Each phase has been included for a reason and should be used for that purpose. Thus, if you alter the images in Phase 3, make sure you are still emphasizing the development of skill in shifting attention from hard to soft eyes, or from a broad to a narrow focus of attention.

This is important because, when you are in the zone, the shifting from a broad to a narrow focus occurs automatically; under pressure, that shifting breaks down. To reduce the likelihood that your ability to shift will break down, you consciously practice it just as you would consciously practice your swing in baseball, or your backhand in tennis. You *overlearn the shifting response*. In addition, no matter how hard you train, you will encounter times when the pressure is so great that automatic shifting simply won't happen. It is at those times that you bite the bullet, or, as Lee Treviño says, "Find a way to get the ball in the hole." At those times, shifting is a very deliberate, forced process. You make yourself do it to get back into the zone.

In general, when you begin taking yourself through the procedures without a tape, you should emphasize the following.

Phase 1

Coordinate the feelings you have when breathing with images of lightness and heaviness. Try to become immersed in those images to actually experience the sensations.

Phase 2

Deepen your level of relaxation by consciously relaxing muscle groups in a standard order:

1. Arms
2. Legs
3. Face
4. Neck and shoulders
5. Chest, back, and abdomen

Some progressive relaxation procedures involve a great deal of structure, beginning with the fingers, hand, forearm, and upper arm of one arm, and then moving to the other arm, and so on. Other procedures start at the toes and move up to the top of the head. Your goal is to shorten the procedures, yet attain a very deep state of relaxation. In my experience with athletes, they are most successful when concentrating first on the extremities. It is quite easy for most athletes to simultaneously relax both arms (including fingers, hands, forearms, and upper arms) with the general instruction, "Relax both arms."

One particular athlete I worked with made the following changes after approximately 3 weeks of training. By that time, he had shortened the entire induction procedure (Phases 1 and 2) to about 3 minutes.

1. First, he would close his eyes and take three breaths, inhaling deeply and exhaling slowly. *This process alone was enough to get him into a light hypnotic state.*
2. Next, he would deepen the state by relaxing both arms and both legs simultaneously. *It would take about 30 seconds for him to feel the level of relaxation he desired.*
3. Finally, he would count from one to five. At this time his focus would be on breathing and relaxing his entire body.
4. After counting he would move directly to Phase 3.

Phase 3

Learn to identify both physical and attentional transition points (these often occur together, but not always). Attentional transition points are those places in the activity (e.g., hitting, throwing, jumping) where you need to shift from one type of attention to another. Most of those shifts will be from a broad-external focus (soft eyes) to a narrow-external focus (hard eyes), or vice versa. A physical transition point is where the distribution of your weight around your center of gravity (the one point) shifts.

For example, a tennis player coming into net momentarily split-steps as he prepares to volley. At this time, his weight is evenly distributed between both feet, and he is balanced, not falling forward (weight in front of the center of gravity) or backward (weight behind the center of gravity). As the player reacts to the ball, the distribution of weight shifts up and down, side to side, or forward and backward. Specifically, as the player punches the volley his weight moves up and forward. This chapter provides several examples of transition points. For a more detailed description of this process, see the section "Difficulty Feeling Centered" in chapter 11.

Phase 3 helps you actually see and feel things as if you were in the particular situation making the shifts. Obviously, this script changes with each performance situation you rehearse. Use this phase to become immersed and to remind yourself of the critical attentional shifts and transition points in your activity.

Phase 4

Develop the feelings and images that occur when you play up to your potential. Really feel the confidence and control. You want to see things as you would when you are playing extremely well, and to feel smooth, coordinated, and strong. Move smoothly through each of the critical transition points in your activity. In this phase you may also begin to practice coping with increasing pressure, changing feelings of anxiety into feelings of confidence.

Phase 5

Practice the procedure you will actually use in the competition (i.e., breathing, saying your trigger words, and refocusing attention). Become immersed in the situation, actually feeling yourself centering and performing. Learn to see things from the perspective of being in a competitive situation. You see them as the participant, not as an observer. During this phase, give yourself the posthypnotic suggestion to center and use your key words in the actual performance situation.

Transition Points by Sport

To develop your own script, your first task involves identifying the critical transition points in your particular sport. To help you begin this process, I have provided a few examples. If your sport is not included here, it's because I lack the coaching expertise to make an exhaustive list. Any coach who is familiar with the biomechanics and the tactical and technical demands of your activity can help you identify the critical transition points of your sport. Use these examples as guides to get the basic idea. Then work out a logical script for your sport based on your particular skill level. For example, an elite diver or gymnast might develop a very complicated script to work through something like a double-twisting, double-back somersault. The script for a simpler move like a front dive or a forward roll would involve fewer transitions.

Baseball/Softball

Hitting.   Attention typically shifts from a broad to a narrow focus as you step into the batter's box. It is internally focused as you dig in and get settled. At this point you are trying to achieve a stable, centered feeling. Attention becomes externally focused once you are settled and may be fairly broad until the pitcher goes into his windup. A transition occurs here as attention narrows on the release point and weight shifts slightly back as you prepare to swing. Weight transfers again as you either step in to swing, or pull away. Attention broadens after the pitch, and the process repeats itself.

Throwing.   Attention is fairly broad until the pitcher goes into his or her windup. Then your weight shifts and attention narrows. You focus on the hitter; your weight drops down a little (you are on your toes) and is centered over both feet (evenly distributed). As the hitter begins to move, your weight starts to shift again to move you in front of the ball. The object is to be quick enough to get in front of the ball and still have enough time to recenter your weight and drop down to field the ball (assuming it's a grounder). As you come up and begin a rocking motion to throw, your weight transfers first toward the back foot and then through the one point and out in front. More skilled players will experience a very quick shift of attention immediately after catching the ball. At this point, attention broadens to check position of runners and make a decision about where to throw the ball. Then attention narrows just before the throw.

Basketball

Free Throws.   Just before you step to the line your attention is fairly broad and externally focused. This allows you to see who is in the game, pick up any signals, and so forth. As you step to the line, attention narrows and becomes internally focused. This focus allows you to check levels of muscle tension and to center yourself, evenly distributing your weight between both feet and feeling slightly lower (i.e., heavier—in more solid contact with the court) than you feel when you are running up and down the court. (Most athletes go through some automatic routine—bouncing the ball three or four times—as they settle in and get centered.) At this time, even though you are bouncing the ball (an automatic response), attention is internally focused as you check feelings and remind yourself of technical cues or strategies. Once you are centered, your attention becomes externally focused on the basket. As you make this attentional transition, you take a deep, centering breath. Knees bend slightly and weight drops lower as you start rocking to transfer your weight up and forward as you take the shot. Immediately after the shot, attention broadens.

Bowling

As you go to pick up your ball, attention is internally focused and fairly broad. At this time you may be reminding yourself of lane conditions, deciding how you want to approach (assuming you are trying to pick up a spare). As you step to the line, a transition occurs in both attention and weight distribution. Attention shifts to a narrow-internal focus as you check your level of muscle tension. You become aware of the feelings in your upper body (shoulders, arms) as you hold the ball in front of you. Once you are comfortable, attention shifts to the pins and to your spot. At this time it is narrowly focused. With the shift comes a centering breath (a partial exhale), and weight transfers slightly forward to compensate for the backswing as you drop the ball and begin your approach. At the top of your backswing, you feel most of your weight on your front leg. Your weight is out in front of your center of mass (to compensate for the heavy ball). As the ball comes through, your weight smoothly shifts back toward the center and upward as you follow through.

Golf

Irons.   As you select your club, attention is shifting from a broad-external focus (to assess course conditions, the position of your ball, etc.) to a broad-internal focus (to make a decision about club selection). As you step up for a practice swing, you shift from a narrow-external focus (to position yourself relative to the ball) to a narrow-internal focus. As you bend down to prepare for a practice swing, your mind is internally focused. You are aware of the tension in your shoulders; you check to see that your weight is centered (evenly distributed over both feet). You check your grip (i.e., how it feels in your hand), the position of your wrists, and so forth. Most golfers have a systematic checklist that they go through. To do this, attention is narrowly focused as you go through each point. (Work out your own checklist with your pro.)

As you prepare for the practice swing, weight will be slightly lower (below your normal center of gravity). That is, you will feel more solid and stable against the ground than you do when you are walking along the course. All golfers have their own preference about how low they will drop their center of mass.

Often a centering breath will help you achieve the proper weight distribution. At the end of that breath you repeat your key words and transfer attention to the ball (narrow-external). At this point you begin your backswing. Weight smoothly transfers upward and toward the back foot, reaching its peak at the top of the backswing. While attention stays focused on the ball and your head is still, weight transfers as the club head changes direction. You can feel your weight (the one point) come down and through the ball with the club. As you follow through, weight shifts forward and up. This is all a very smooth motion. Talk yourself through this Phase 3. Because this is a conscious process you do it a little at a time. In Phase 4 you put it together and let yourself feel it happen in real time. You don't talk, just feel.

Creating a Script

You have all the tools you need to develop the control that will allow you to play much closer to your full potential. Your motivation, enthusiasm, and your willingness to make choices and commit to practice will determine the success or failure of your efforts. The following pages provide some additional scripts for Phases 3, 4, and 5 to use as models for your own tapes. Feel free to make modifications in the scripts to suit your personal needs. The process goes more smoothly if you are comfortable with the words used in the script.

The following scripts are based on the transition points from several different sports. This should provide you with some examples to use as you fill in the details of your Phases 3, 4, and 5.

Hitting in Baseball

PHASE 3

Now, imagine that you are in the batting circle preparing to hit. . . . You take a few practice swings and you watch the pitcher. . . . You notice his delivery, . . . and you begin timing your practice swings with his delivery as if you were the batter. . . . You adopt a hitting position, watch the pitcher release the ball, . . . and swing as you see it cross the plate . . . . That's fine. . . . .

Begin your walk to the plate. . . . Feel yourself take that first step out of the batting circle. . . . Feel the weight of the bat in your hands as you let it drop to your side. . . . Notice how comfortable the bat feels in your hand. . . . Solid. . . . Firm. . . . It's a feeling that gives you confidence. . . . The bat feels strong and powerful in your hands.

Step into the batter's box and begin digging in. . . . Take your time, get your back foot into a position that feels comfortable, feel the slight bend in your back knee. . . . Now, position your front foot and take your normal practice swing. . . . As you take your practice swing, take a deep, centering breath. . . . Breathe from your abdomen. . . . On the exhale . . . relax neck and shoulder muscles. . . .

As you exhale and relax your neck and shoulder muscles, let your attention broaden so that you see the entire playing field. . . . At the same time, remind yourself that you are _____ and _____ [insert trigger words here].

As you exhale and relax your neck and shoulder muscles, let your attention broaden so that you see the entire playing field. . . . Remind yourself that you are _____ and _____ .

As the pitcher goes into his windup, you inhale slightly. . . . As you do, . . . your concentration becomes focused on the release point. . . . As the pitcher goes into his windup, you inhale slightly. . . . As you do, . . . your concentration becomes focused on the release point. You see the ball come out of his hand. . . . You pick up the rotation, . . . you see the seams. . . . It's your pitch. . . . You can feel your weight begin to shift to your back foot as you begin the motion that starts your swing. At the same time your arms come back slightly as you get cocked. . . . Watch the ball. . . . Dig in. . . . Come through. . . . That's fine.

PHASE 4

Good. . . . Now take your time. . . . Rehearse two at-bats. . . . Let the count in one of those at-bats get to 3 and 2. . . . Practice feeling yourself in the batter's box. . . . Practice controlling the pace of things. . . . Don't let the pitcher rush you. . . . Step out if you aren't ready. . . . Each time you step into the box, dig in, . . . take a centering breath, . . . relax, and see the whole field. . . . As the pitcher winds up, . . . inhale slightly. . . . Focus concentration on the release of the ball. . . . Good. . . . Now rehearse two good at-bats. . . . Protect the plate. . . . Look for your pitch. . . .

LEAVE TIME FOR REHEARSAL HERE.

PHASE 5

That's fine. . . . In a moment it will be time to leave this pleasant state of hypnosis. . . . Before you do, . . . you need to know that you will be able to create the feelings of being _____ and _____ [insert trigger words here] when you are about to bat by stepping into the batter's box and taking a deep breath. . . . On the exhale . . . say to your-self, _____ and _____ . On the exhale . . . say to your-self, _____ and _____ . You will be able to create the feelings of being _____ and _____ when you are about to bat. . . . Step into the batter's box. . . . Take a deep breath. . . . On the exhale . . . say to yourself, _____ and _____ . . . . Remember, . . . whenever you want to settle yourself down and improve concentration, . . . you simply take a deep, centering breath. . . . On the exhale say _____ and _____ .

Imagine yourself going through that process now. . . . Imagine you are about to step into the batter's box. . . . You are feeling a little tight. . . . You are worried about the possibility of striking out. . . . As you step into the batter's box, dig in; . . . take that deep, centering breath; . . . and say your key words. . . . As you step into the batter's box, dig in; . . . take that deep, centering breath; . . . and say your key words. . . . You can feel yourself relax. You can feel the strength and power in your bat. . . . As the pitcher goes into his windup, focus attention on the release point. . . . Pick up the ball as it comes out of his hand. . . .

Alright, . . . it's time to return to your normal activities. . . . To do that, count from three to one. On the count of three take a deep breath, . . . holding it momentarily. . . . On two stretch your arms and legs and exhale. . . . On one open your eyes and you will be wide awake, ready to do the things that you normally do at this time. . . . You're feeling good, comfortable, and relaxed. . . . Ready. . . . Three, . . . take a deep breath. . . . Two, . . . stretch your arms and legs and exhale. . . . One, . . . open your eyes, wide awake!

It is important to remember that listening to the tape of this script will be different from the things you experience in the batter's box. In these sessions, you consciously practice feeling your weight shift, attending to the feel of the bat in your hands, and so forth. At the plate, you consciously attend to breathing, relaxing muscles, and saying your key words. Then, your attention is focused on the release of the ball, and you simply let everything that follows happen. You don't talk your way through it; you let your body automatically do what your mental practice has prepared it to do.

Putting in Golf

PHASE 3

That's fine. . . . Now imagine that you are reaching into your golf bag and pulling out your putter. . . . Look at the bag. . . . Notice where the putter is. . . . Feel its shape as you grab it, . . . pulling it out of the bag. . . . Walk around the green, . . . checking for anything that might interfere with your putt. . . . Take your time. . . . Now move behind the ball and try to line up the putt. . . . Check the break of the green. . . . Pick the spot just in front of your ball that you are going to use to line up with the hole. . . .

As you straighten up, feel it in your legs . . . and back. . . . If it's normal for you to take a second look, . . . do so. . . . As soon as you are ready, move up to a position by the ball. . . . Look down and check the position of your feet relative to the ball. . . . Check the distribution of your weight. . . . Is it evenly distributed between your two feet? . . . Inhale deeply from your abdomen as you start to bend over for a practice stroke. . . . As you partially exhale, let your shoulders and arms relax. . . . Feel your weight drop down slightly. . . . Feel the bend in your knees as your club head drops into position for your practice stroke. . . . Look just ahead to the spot where you are going to putt your ball. . . . As you look back to your ball, take an easy, centering breath. When you have exhaled to the point where you are comfortable, remind yourself that you feel _____ and _____ [insert trigger words here]. . . . As you look back to your ball, take an easy, centering breath. When you have exhaled to the point where you are comfortable, remind yourself that you feel _____ and _____ . . . . Take your practice putt. . . .

Good. . . . Now, . . . step up to the ball. . . . Check your spot. . . . Center, and, as you drop your club head into position to stroke the ball, remind yourself that you feel _____ and _____ . . . . Stroke the putt.

Some golfers like to substitute a technical or process cue for either the physical cue word or the psychological cue word (e.g., easy and head still). Talk over possible cue words with your teaching pro.

PHASE 4

Good. . . . Now, take your time. . . . Rehearse a few putts. Rehearse every aspect of the putt. . . . Try putts of different lengths and with different breaks. . . . Make some of them easy and some more difficult. . . . Imagine that other golfers are present, but don't let them rush you. . . . Notice how the focus of your concentration shifts from a broad focus as you look around the entire green . . . to a very narrow focus as you line up the putt and stroke the ball. . . . Use your centering and your key words. . . . Practice now. . . .

LEAVE TIME FOR REHEARSAL HERE.

PHASE 5

That's fine. . . . In a moment it will be time to leave this pleasant state of hypnosis. . . . Before you do, . . . you need to know that you will be able to create the feelings of being _____ and _____ [insert trigger words here] *when you are about to putt by stepping up to the ball . . . and taking a deep breath. . . . On the exhale . . . say to yourself, "_____ and _____ ." On the exhale . . . say to yourself, "_____ and _____ ." You will be able to create the feelings of being _____ and _____ when you are about to putt. . . . Step up to the ball. . . . Take a deep breath. . . . On the exhale . . . say to yourself, "_____ and _____ ." Remember, . . . whenever you want to settle yourself down and improve concentration, . . . you simply take a deep, centering breath. . . . On the exhale say "_____ and _____ ."*

Imagine yourself going through that process now. . . . Imagine you are about to putt. . . . You are feeling a little tight. . . . You want this one. . . . You start to worry about losing a stroke. . . . You can stop your worrying by taking a centering breath and saying your key words. . . . As you step up to the ball, . . . take that centering breath . . . and say your key words. . . . Feel yourself relax. . . . Feel the confidence in your hands and in your putter. . . . Stroke the putt. . . .

Alright. . . . It's time to return to your normal activities. . . . To do that, count from three to one. On the count of three take a deep breath, . . . holding it momentarily. . . . On the count of two stretch your arms and legs and exhale. . . . On the count of one open your eyes and you will be wide awake, ready to do the things that you normally do at this time. . . .

*You're feeling good, comfortable, and relaxed. . . . Ready. . . .
Three, . . . take a deep breath. . . . Two, . . . stretch your arms
and legs and exhale. . . . One, . . . open your eyes, wide awake!*

Controlling Negative Thinking From Fatigue[1]

PHASE 3

*Imagine that you are running a race, and you are performing
very well. . . . You have reached the last stage of the race,
and you are still feeling strong. . . . You look around and
notice that a couple of people are still with you. . . . In
fact, one of them has a slight lead. . . . You can tell from
their expressions and their movements that they are very
tired. . . . They are fighting the fatigue. . . .*

*You have reached a point in the race where it's time to
make a move. . . . You sense that the person behind you
recognizes this, too. . . . As you reach this point, . . . you take
an extra deep, . . . centering breath. . . . On the exhale you
say to yourself, "_____ and _____"* [insert trigger words
here]. *Just as you finish saying "_____ and _____," your
concentration narrows and you make your move. . . . The
person behind you begins to sprint, too. . . . You are so
focused, you don't really notice. . . . You feel so strong and
confident that you don't worry about the outcome of the
race. . . . That confidence frees you to focus your attention on
the power you feel in your arms and legs as you make your
move. . . . You can feel yourself dig in and pull. . . . You feel
solid, . . . strong. . . .*

*You see the finish. . . . As you do, your concentration is
focused on a point just beyond the finish as you drive. . . .
You see yourself passing the leader, . . . pulling away from
everyone, . . . and winning the race. . . .*

PHASE 4

*That's fine. . . . Now, run the final stages of a race. . . . Let
your imagination go. . . . Get completely involved in the race.*

---

[1]Coping with fatigue and maintaining form and concentration when you are tired is an
important concern in all sports. This running example can be adapted to your particular
sport.

. . . Imagine that you are running at an even pace. . . . Your attention is fairly broad, and you are aware of the course and the positions of your competition. . . . You are relaxed, but getting tired. . . . You are coming to a critical point in the race, . . . a point where either you . . . or your competition will make a move. . . . As you are about to reach that point, you find yourself having negative thoughts. . . . You begin to wonder if you have enough left. . . . Your thoughts serve as a trigger. . . . They remind you that everyone is tired. . . . They remind you to . . . take a centering breath . . . and use your key words. . . . "I feel _____ and _____ ." At the end of the exhale, . . . your attention narrows, . . . and you sprint. . . . You are focused on either the finish, . . . or the one technical cue that will help you get the most out of yourself (e.g., muscle tension and lean) [You and your coach should determine what that focus should be.] *Alright, take some time to become completely involved in your run. . . . Rehearse every aspect of it. . . .*

LEAVE 2 MINUTES HERE FOR REHEARSAL.

PHASE 5

That's fine. . . . In a moment it will be time to leave this pleasant state of hypnosis. . . . Before you do, . . . you need to know that you will be able to stop negative thinking . . . and to create the feelings of being _____ and _____ [insert trigger words here] *when you are in a race by taking a deep breath. . . . On the exhale . . . say to yourself, "_____ and _____ ." On the exhale say to yourself, "_____ and _____ ." You will be able to create the feelings of being _____ and _____ when you are in a race by taking a deep breath. . . . On the exhale . . . say to yourself, "_____ and _____ ." Remember, . . . whenever you want to settle yourself down and improve concentration, . . . you simply take a deep, centering breath. . . . On the exhale say "_____ and _____ ."*

Imagine yourself going through that process now. . . . Imagine you are tired, and the negative thoughts start coming in. . . . You feel yourself beginning to tighten up. . . . You are worried about the possibility of losing. . . . As you reach that critical stage in the race, take a deep, centering breath . . . and say your key words. . . . As you reach that critical stage in the race, take a deep, centering breath . . . and say your key words. . . . You can feel yourself relax. . . . You can feel the strength and power return. . . .

Alright. . . . It's time to return to your normal activities. . . . To do that, count from three to one. On the count of three take a deep breath, . . . holding it momentarily. . . . On the count of two stretch your arms and legs and exhale. . . . On the count of one open your eyes and you will be wide awake, ready to do the things that you normally do at this time. . . . You're feeling good, comfortable, and relaxed. . . . Ready. . . . Three, . . . take a deep breath. . . . Two, . . . stretch your arms and legs and exhale. . . . One, . . . open your eyes, wide awake!

CHAPTER 11

A TROUBLESHOOTER'S GUIDE: CONQUERING THE UNEXPECTED IN MENTAL TRAINING

Imagine your name is Reggie Jackson and you have a chance to win a World Series game. If you get your pitch, you know it's going out of the park.

Although you probably won't have any problems with your own training program, issues do develop from time to time that can slow down your progress. This chapter outlines some of the rough spots that people occasionally encounter as they attempt to learn self-hypnosis.

If you aren't experiencing any difficulties in your own program, you needn't proceed any further in this chapter. The following pages list some of the problems that occur and makes some suggestions for dealing with them.

Difficulty Getting the Pendulum to Move

A small number of people have difficulty getting the pendulum to move. Each of these people fights an internal battle: One part of the person wants the pendulum to move, and the other part doesn't. If this seems to be your problem, stop trying to get the pendulum to move; instead, simply observe it and describe what happens. Often this letting go resolves the conflict. What usually happens is that the pendulum begins to move slightly in a circle. As you let go and watch to see what happens, the movement will increase.

Another thing to check is the position of your wrist. It should be bent, and the muscles should be relaxed. Also, make sure that you are holding the string firmly, but not too tightly. It's a gentle firmness—tight enough to keep from dropping the pendulum, but not so tight that you crush the string.

It sometimes takes several tries before you gain control over the pendulum. In fact, many people go on to learn self-hypnosis before they get the pendulum to move (it's not a prerequisite to learning self-hypnosis). After having learned to let their imaginations go and to become immersed in the images they create, they are able to come back to the pendulum and get it to move.

Difficulty Feeling Centered and Feeling the Shifts in Your Center of Mass

If you are having difficulty feeling centered, try the following exercise. Sit up in a chair with your back straight and your feet flat on the floor (see Figure 11.1). Your center of mass is indicated by the white square in the middle of the person in Figure 11.1. As you sit in the chair, you should feel most of your weight pressing down toward the floor in the direction of the arrow located under the chair.

Now, as you are sitting in that position, imagine how you would react if someone came sneaking up behind you and suddenly shouted "BOO!" Notice what happens to your breathing, to the muscle tension in your neck and shoulders, and to the feeling you have about your weight distribution.

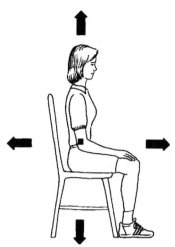

Figure 11.1
Finding your center of mass.

If you reacted like most people, you probably found yourself inhaling from up in your chest and momentarily holding your breath. At the same time, you should have noticed the tension in chest, neck, and shoulder muscles increasing. These two changes typically result in a slight upward shift in your center of mass. You can feel more of your weight moving, in the direction of the arrow above the person's head in Figure 11.1.

If you didn't experience this sequence of changes, try it again, only this time, consciously inhale, expanding your lungs instead of your diaphragm, and momentarily hold your breath. Increase the tension in the muscles in your chest, neck, and shoulders. If you do that, you should feel the shift in your center of mass. That shift is what I am talking about when I say that athletes become too tense and feel unsteady (i.e., like a triangle on its head).

Now, I want you to feel what it is like when you become too relaxed. Sitting in the chair, imagine that you are very tired. Don't allow yourself to lean back against the back of the chair. Just imagine that you are very tired. You have just finished a long run, or some other vigorous exercise, and you are trying to catch your breath.

Take a few seconds to create that image, and see what happens to the distribution of your weight around your center of mass. Did it shift downward, in the direction of the arrow under the chair? Did you find yourself feeling heavy and lethargic, as if it would be difficult to move?

If you didn't feel that shift when you just thought about being tired, take yourself through the actual behaviors. Sitting in the chair without leaning back, relax muscles in neck, shoulders, chest, and stomach. As you do this, your shoulders will slump as if it's just too difficult to resist the pull of gravity. Inhale deeply as if you were catching your breath. As you exhale you should be able to feel more of your weight pressing down against the chair and toward the floor. You should feel heavier, too heavy if you were going to try to react quickly to an opponent.

I have two more exercises for you. Once again, sit up straight in the chair. Your weight should feel more centered, neither too high, nor too low. If this is the case, you should feel a bit more ready, neither too tense, nor too relaxed.

Once you feel that way, imagine that you are listening to someone talk. Imagine a situation in which you are extremely interested in the subject and trying to hear every word. As you get into that image, what happens to weight in relation to your center of mass?

Under the conditions just described, most of us find ourselves straightening up just a bit and leaning forward. If that happened you should have experienced a shifting of your weight forward. You should feel your weight move in the direction of the arrow located in front of the person in Figure 11.1. More of your weight is now out in front of your center of mass.

In this last exercise, imagine a scene in which you are feeling a little annoyed with the person who is talking (lecturing) to you. You feel it is useless to argue, and you don't really want to be there. Once again, what happened to your weight distribution? Under the conditions just described, many people literally shift away from the person talking. You can feel that shift by noticing that more of your weight feels distributed behind the one point, or in back of your center of mass.

The baseball player in Figure 11.1 shows what happens in an actual sport setting. If the baseball player in the figure is standing in the batter's box and feeling anxious and tense, he is likely to be a bit unsteady. He may be aware of the tension in his neck and shoulders and at the same time have difficulty feeling solid or steady in the batter's box. In other words, he is much more tuned in to the feelings in his upper body than he is to the feelings in his lower body. At this point, weight may be distributed evenly between both feet, but more of his feelings are above the one point.

Now, the same batter is in the batter's box. It has been a long practice and he is tired. As soon as he finishes up he can go home. His motivation level (for hitting) is at an all-time low. He just wants to get it over with. Under these conditions, the batter is probably more aware of the feelings in his lower body. His weight may be evenly distributed between his feet, but he feels heavy, as if more of his weight were closer to the ground.

Next, imagine that you are a confident hitter. Perhaps your name is Reggie Jackson, and you have a chance to win a World Series game. There are two men on base and two outs. You decide that if you get your pitch, it's going out of the park. You feel centered and ready. As you watch the pitcher release the ball, you know it's your pitch. You feel your weight shift slightly to your back foot as you prepare to swing. You are aggressive, and this means you will go after the pitch. The slight shift backward allowed you to shift your weight forward, getting it through the ball as your bat makes contact. As you begin your swing you can feel that weight shifting, moving through the one point and on out in front as you follow through. Pow! Out of the park.

The reverse occurs when you are intimidated or defensive. Your team is behind by a run. It's two out and bottom of the ninth. You are the worst hitter on the team—the last person who should be in this situation. The pitcher is overpowering, and you are praying for a miracle.

As you stand in the batter's box, your weight is likely to be slightly above and in front of your center of mass. As the pitcher goes into his windup, your tendency will be to begin to fall away, that is, to have your weight begin to fall backward behind the one point.

The difference between you and Reggie Jackson is that you aren't shifting the weight to attack. Rather, you are shifting to give yourself more time—to get away from the pitch. Seeing that the ball will be over the plate, you attempt to swing, but as you do, you are still falling backwards. Under these conditions you either miss, or dribble the ball into the infield.

Exercises like these can help make you more aware of your center of mass. If you have had difficulty feeling the movements during your self-hypnosis sessions, take the time to actually walk through the activities, calling your attention to weight distribution at each stage.

Difficulty Establishing a Feeling of Lightness in Your Arm

As I indicated in chapter 9, learning to develop feelings of lightness and heaviness in your arm can be very valuable. Unfortunately, developing the feeling of lightness is not that easy for some people. If you find that you are having difficulty getting your arm to feel light and to float up as you take yourself through the hypnotic procedure, don't force it!

The primary purpose for the arm levitation procedure is to help you deepen your hypnotic state. To the extent that you are able to become immersed in the images of lightness and that your arm begins to rise, this will happen. Unfortunately, if your arm does not rise and you get into a battle with yourself trying to make it rise, you don't deepen your hypnotic state, you weaken it.

For purposes of induction, it is more important to avoid conflict. Thus, if your arm doesn't feel light, react passively or unemotionally to that fact. Move away from that set of suggestions and focus on something you do feel. For instance, many people find it quite easy to create the feeling of heaviness. If that is true for you, then focus on this feeling. Spend a little more time on the development of heaviness and move right from this suggestion into the counting procedure.

A second alternative is to substitute some imagined scene that you find relaxing for the arm levitation part of the procedure. You may find, for example, that you can create a general feeling of lightness by imagining you are floating on a cloud or on an air mattress in a swimming pool. Make sure the image you select is relaxing and nonthreatening.

As you gain confidence and experience at developing the self-hypnotic state you can return to the task of getting your arm to float. Just be patient, and don't push for things to happen too quickly. If you can do that, your patience will be rewarded.

Feeling a Sense of Anxiety or Panic as You Become More Deeply Hypnotized

For the majority of people, becoming hypnotized is a very relaxing and enjoyable experience. Some people find that as they begin to give up control and let themselves go, they begin to feel anxious. If you find that happening, stop what you are doing.

In most instances, there is a good reason for the anxiety that develops. Typically, however, that reason isn't immediately apparent to the person who is feeling the anxiety. If you wish to continue with your program, work with a psychologist who can help you discover the reason for the anxiety and then get you past that temporary block. This usually requires only two or three sessions.

Problems With Key Words

Perhaps the biggest problem surrounding key words is that people expect them to magically change the feelings they are having at a given moment. If this is your problem, you need to realize that you have to work at making the words automatic responses. This is why mastering self-hypnosis is so important— it helps you overlearn responses. This makes it more likely that you will remember to use your key words at critical times. Overlearning responses helps you control anxiety enough to possibly avoid a crisis and thereby gradually regain control. It won't instantly get rid of every bit of anxiety.

Remember, using key words helps you gain control over concentration and tension during those times when you are not performing well. When you are in the zone, the last thing you need to do is consciously try to get in the zone. You are immersed in the competitive experience to the point where you are reacting automatically without having to consciously remind yourself of things. Key words are designed to help you make the transition from being out of control to gradually getting into the zone. Using your key words is a conscious process. While you are consciously attending to the key words, you can't be in the zone.

Your key words are potent reminders to get you to make changes in muscle tension and focus on concentration. In that sense, they are not unlike instructions a swimmer might give herself to lengthen her stroke. At first, the process of lengthening the stroke is conscious, the swimmer must work at focusing attention on the mechanics of making necessary changes. Gradually, however, a rhythm is established and the swimmer's attention is freed from having to think about her stroke. At this point she is on automatic, and using her key words has become part of that automatic process. She didn't snap her fingers and get there—she had to work at it.

As you discipline yourself to use the procedures and gain control over tension levels and distractions, you will see a gradual change in the consistency of your performance. You will also see a gradual increase in your ability to control your physical and mental responses. The frequency, intensity, and duration of mistakes will all be reduced, but they will never be totally eliminated. The best way to deal with this is to *set more realistic goals.*

Difficulty Staying Focused on Process as Opposed to Outcome

Winning and losing are important emotional issues to highly competitive athletes. Learning to set these concerns aside when they interfere with performance is extremely difficult. You can't expect to change overnight those behaviors that have been with you for years, so you must set realistic goals. The following guidelines will help you stick with your training program, especially when you become discouraged.

1. *Focus your attention on what you should, and not what you shouldn't, be doing.* It does no good to tell yourself *not* to worry about winning. That is an impossible challenge. If I said to you right now, "Don't think about sex for the next 2 minutes," you couldn't do it! Think I'm wrong? Try it!

Instead of worrying about what not to do, constantly refocus attention on positive instructions, like "Watch the ball," "Loose and easy," "Breathe," and "Follow through." In other words, direct attention to positive cues, without arguing with yourself about what you should or shouldn't be thinking.

2. *Set reasonable goals.* The greater the pressure you feel, the more interference you can expect. Thus you will find yourself having to work to reestablish control more frequently. Set goals to reduce the duration and frequency of your distractions. But leave any goals related to outcome, such as winning, behind. Focusing on those goals will only interfere with the learning process. Work first on reducing the duration of your excessive tension and mental distractions. Distractions will occur; speed of recovery is the critical variable. Set reasonable goals for improving your recovery time by monitoring how long it currently takes you to recover under several different levels of pressure.

3. *Seek the support of people around you to help you reestablish priorities within the actual sport situation.* Too often, teammates, coaches, parents, and other well-meaning individuals can sabotage your training program. You see, outcome is the primary focus for these people, too. Even when they want to help you get away from that focus, they have a tendency (especially under pressure) to draw you back to it. Your coach's behavior reminds you that outcome matters. To help you, critical others have to be willing to work on the issue with you and find ways to remind themselves and you of newly established goals. If you do that, winning will take care of itself.

4. *Make a commitment to remind yourself of your goals while you're away from the practice and competitive settings.* Being your very best means making a total commitment to mentally rehearsing and practicing your procedures. Surround yourself with notes on doors and walls and pictures that support you and remind you to work on your program.

Failure to Remember to Use Procedures in Practice or Competition

Many athletes find it difficult to follow through on a program. For some, that failure is due to a lack of motivation. For others, it is due to too much motivation. Still others are so enthusiastic about learning and about trying new things that they just can't stay focused. Their minds are too active, and they jump from one thing to another. Finally, some athletes worry so much under pressure that even things they have drilled through their heads seem to disappear.

If you have the motivation, but also have an enthusiastic mind or a tendency to forget things under pressure, then you might need to rely on external reminders. First, turn over some control to critical others (e.g., coaches or teammates), allowing them to find ways to remind you what you are working on during practice and competitions.

When this isn't possible, or when you want to be able to remind yourself, you can make use of a simple device called an *intention-arousing device* (IAD).[1] The IAD is nothing more than a countdown timer, approximately 2 inches by 2 inches square and 1/2-inch thick, which clips to your pocket or belt. It repeatedly times any interval you choose from 1 minute to 24 hours. At the end of the interval a small vibrator in the device is activated for about 2 seconds. You are the only one aware of the vibration. It serves as a stimulus to remind you of whatever it is you are working on (e.g., to be aggressive or to think positive thoughts). Typically, the higher the level of anxiety, and the more susceptible you are to distractions due to enthusiasm, the shorter the time interval you set (2-3 minutes is a common interval for many athletes).

Conclusion

Congratulations. Having made it this far, you have demonstrated the kind of commitment required to play in the zone more often. If you can be patient and remember that self-confidence and faith come through commitment in the face of doubts, you'll gain the mental edge you're looking for. It's up to you now. You have the knowledge you need, and with that knowledge you, too, can become the performer you've only ever dreamed of becoming.

---

[1]The IAD is marketed under the trade name of "Motiv Aider" and is available from Behavioral Dynamics, Inc., Box 66, Thief River Falls, MN 56701.

GLOSSARY

altered state of consciousness (ASC)—The change in awareness when there is a breakdown in the shifting of your focus of attention from internal thoughts and feelings to external stimuli.

anxiety—Feelings and thoughts associated with doubt and worry. Words suggestive of anxiety include panicked, worried, tenseness, tightness, nervous, upset, confused, overloaded, pressured, and rushed.

attention—*See* concentration.

belief—A view you hold (e.g., "I will win") until you are confronted with objective evidence to the contrary.

bracing—A generalized increase in muscle tension often associated with anxiety or an increased level of arousal.

centered—A confident state you can achieve immediately before performing that lets you know with certainty you are mentally and physically ready.

centering—A breathing technique designed to produce physical balance and mental focus.

center of gravity—*See* center of mass.

center of mass—Also referred to as *center of gravity* and *one point*. Your center of mass is located slightly behind your navel. You can locate your center of mass by imagining two lines drawn through your body, one vertical and one horizontal. The lines intersected at your midpoint, or center of mass.

concentration—The act of paying attention. There are four different focuses of concentration: broad-external, broad-internal, narrow-external, and narrow-internal. Most performance situations require the shifting of attention from one focus to another. Thus, control over concentration requires control over both the width (broad or narrow) and direction (internal or external) of attention.

choking—When attention becomes so focused on internal cues (thoughts and feelings) that you cannot attend to external task-relevant cues.

consciousness—Awareness of thoughts (words, images) that you control. Silently talking through a performance, systematically rehearsing movements in your mind, or mentally arguing about the best way to do something are conscious processes.

faith—A view you hold even in the face of objective evidence to the contrary (e.g., still believing you can win when the score is against you or you are outclassed by the opposition). Faith is not absolute, but a matter of degree. You build faith by forcing yourself to behave as if you hold a view, even when you don't.

hallucinogens—Chemicals like lysergic acid (LSD), dimethyltryptamine (DMT), mescaline, and marijuana that affect attentional processes and information processing and storage. Hallucinogens result in abnormal perceptions by breaking down the normal shifting of attention and reducing the brain's ability to inhibit sensory input.

hard eyes—A characteristic of concentration that narrows the focus of attention. Pupils are more constricted, and you lose awareness of objects farther out in the visual field. You use this focus in "going for broke," putting everything you have into an effort.

hyperresponsivity—Hypersuggestibility during self-hypnosis. I prefer *hyperresponsivity* because it implies that you are in control, choosing to respond.

ideomotor response—A physical movement that occurs without conscious effort in response to a thought. Ideomotor responses can either interfere with or facilitate performance.

immersion—Becoming absorbed in thought, or performance, when there is a breakdown in the shifting of attention. Immersion may be internal (in thoughts or feelings) or external (in the events going on around you), and it is judged as "positive" or "negative" depending on the performance relevance of your attentional focus.

inner voice—Self-talk that results in shifting attention from an external to an internal focus; it may lead to ideomotor responses as well.

irrational belief—A view that is contrary to fact. We infer that an athlete has an irrational belief on the basis of behavior. For example, the inability to accept anything less than perfection implies an individual believes he or she must be perfect. Since athletes are human beings, such beliefs often lead to unhappiness, frustration, and performance problems.

key words—*See* trigger words.

mental rehearsal—The systematic practice in the mind of some performer, involving the imagination across all senses (sights, sounds, touches, tastes, smells). The rehearsal process as used here requires the athlete to assume the role of performer as opposed to observer.

one point—*See* center of mass.

overlearning—Practicing a skill well beyond the point of acquisition so as to develop automatic performance, the ability to perform in the face of pressure or distractions.

peak experience—An altered state of consciousness associated with performing at an automatic level, without having to consciously think about the things you are doing. *See also* playing in the zone.

playing in the zone—Alterations in normal perception that result in greater feelings of control and a slowed sense of time. When playing in the zone, you pay more attention to external task-relevant cues and play at a more unconscious level than usual.

posthypnotic suggestion—An instruction given in hypnosis or self-hypnosis to be acted upon during the normal waking state.

self-confidence—A situation-specific feeling of assurance about performing well.

self-esteem—One's general view of self-worth and ability. An athlete with high self-esteem is generally self-confident.

self-hypnosis—A self-induced state of relaxation that enhances your ability to respond to your own suggestions. Self-hypnosis is a tool to increase your ability to get immersed in what you attend to.

soft eyes—A characteristic of concentration associated with a broad-external focus of attention that allows you to be sensitive to movement in the periphery and to anticipate movement of others.

tension—Physiological tenseness in muscles. *Tight* and *loose* are the terms typically used to describe the feelings associated with muscle tension levels.

trigger words—Cue words used to create desired physical and psychological feelings in a performance situation.

unconsciousness—Any automatic process. Any behavior that you can engage in without having to think about is unconscious. Most motor behaviors, once they are initiated, are completed without conscious thought. You consciously attend to motor sequences (e.g., hitting, serving, jumping) only when you want to make a change in technique.

weight transfer—The shifting of weight around your center of mass.

REFERENCES AND SUGGESTED READINGS

Barber, T.X. (Ed.) (1976). *Advances in altered states of consciousness & human potentialities, Vol. 1.* New York: Psychological Dimensions.

Hackfort, D., & Spielberger, C.D. (Eds.) (1989). *Anxiety in sports: An international perspective.* New York: Hemisphere Publishing.

Ludwig, A. (1969). Altered states of consciousness. In C. Tart (Ed.), *Altered states of consciousness* (pp. 9-22). New York: John Wiley & Sons.

Martens, R. (1990). *Competitive anxiety in sport.* Champaign, IL: Human Kinetics.

Nideffer, R.M. (1970). *The inner athlete.* New York: Crowell.

Nideffer, R.M. (1985). *Athletes' guide to mental training.* Champaign, IL: Human Kinetics.

Ornstein, R.E. (Ed.) (1973). *The nature of human consciousness.* San Francisco: W.H. Freeman & Co.

Sargent, W. (1957). *Battle for the mind.* Baltimore: Penguin Books.

Soskis, D.A. (1986). *Teaching self-hypnosis: An introductory guide for clinicians.* New York: Norton.

INDEX

ABOUT THE AUTHOR

Dr. Robert Nideffer is one of America's premier sport psychologists. He developed the techniques in *Psyched to Win* during his work with the 1984 and 1988 U.S. Olympic teams and in his private practice. Dr. Nideffer is the author of more than a dozen books, including *Athletes' Guide to Mental Training* from Human Kinetics; serves on the editorial board of such prestigious journals as the *Journal of Sport & Exercise Psychology* and *The Physician and Sportsmedicine*; and is president of Enhanced Performance Systems. He earned his PhD in clinical and experimental psychology from Vanderbilt University.

Dr. Nideffer has worked with the Australian Institute for Sport, the Coaching Association of Canada, and the U.S., Canadian, and Australian Olympic teams. In addition to athletes, he is a consultant to multinational corporations, police forces, and the military. In *Psyched to Win*, he shares with you the mental training techniques that he has used so successfully with many of the world's finest athletes.